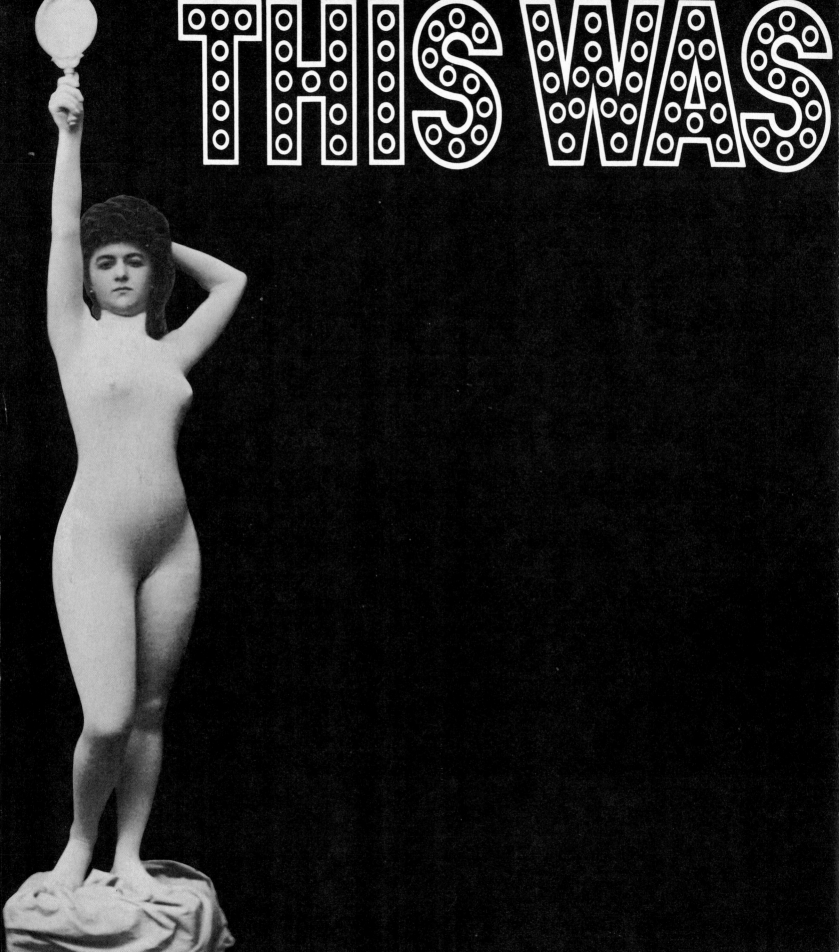

THIS WAS

BURLESQUE

by

ANN CORIO

with

Joseph DiMona

Madison Square Press
Grosset & Dunlap, publishers, New York

Book designed by Martin Rosenzweig

This book is dedicated
to
Michael P. Iannucci,
whose faith, determination, and ingenuity
made possible the show,
This Was Burlesque.

Contents

Setting the pattern

Here come the girls!

IS BURLESQUE BAWDY? YES. IS IT LOVA-ble? Yes. Is it durable? Most decidedly yes. It's been with us one hundred years in this country, and its roots go all the way back to ancient Greece.

Few people know the real story of burlesque, and that's one reason I'm writing this book. They don't realize that burlesque for centuries has been a legitimate branch of show business. I'll admit it's the lowest branch, but that's the limb nearest the people. Its ancestral father was one of the greatest classic playwrights of all time, Aristophanes.

Aristophanes was the first to satirize people, human tragedies, and contemporary ideas and events. He laughed at the world in his plays, and he made people laugh, too. And that's what burlesque means. It comes from the Italian word *burlare,* which means "to laugh at, to make fun of."

In *Lysistrata,* for example, the heroine organized a women's peace association (oh, how a modern burlesque comic would love *that* name). The association was composed of the wives of Athenian warriors, who shut themselves up in the Acropolis away from their husbands until the Peloponnesian War was terminated. What they were saying, two thousand years before the hippies, was, "Make love, not war."

Aristophanes freely used puns, gags, and wisecracks in his plays. What's more, he played up sensual descriptions and introduced the seduction theme into the theatre. The risqué elements that have always been a part of burlesque can also be credited to old Aristophanes, who must have been quite a character around the Acropolis. Where was *he* during the Peloponnesian War? He wasn't making war.

Burlesque first appeared in the English language in a play entitled *The Most Lamentable Comedy and Most Cruel Death of Pyramus and Thisbie,* produced in London in 1600. It set the pattern for all the lusty satires and parodies to follow.

Of these, the most famous may be *The Beggar's Opera,* by John Gay. First produced at the Lincoln's Inn Theatre in 1727, it apparently tore old London town apart. The Archbishop of Canterbury preached a sermon against it; Sir John Fielding, the Police Justice, officially begged the manager not to present it on Saturday evenings, as it would "inspire the idle apprentices of London, who see it on their night off, to imitate its heroes' thieving deeds." Someone named Dr. Wharton condemned it as "the parent of that most monstrous of all absurdities, the comic opera."

Needless to say, with notices like these, the play was a smash; and in 1750 it traveled to the New World. In those days in New York you had to shoulder Indians aside to get into a theatre, but thousands of Americans did. It was presented at a theatre on Nassau Street as a "play written in ridicule of the musical Italian drama."

What with one war and another, American playwrights didn't get on the ball until almost seventy-five years later. But when they did, they ran with it. One of the great, little-known talents in the history of the theatre is a playwright named John Brougham. At the time he was called the American Aristophanes.

No wonder. This man had a way with words and a genius for comedy. He delighted in taking Shakespearian classics, as well as current dramas of the time, and burlesquing them. He was so successful that such actors as the great Edwin Booth would often journey downtown to recreate their legitimate roles in a Brougham spoof.

When they didn't, other actors would do the job for them, as an actor named Forrest learned to his regret. Forrest was appearing in a legitimate play uptown, while his burlesque counterpart imitated him downtown. Listen to this report:

Lysistrata, with Sydney Greenstreet (*center*) and company

As Beppo, *made up in a very clever imitation of Forrest as the Gladiator, and enormously padded, he strutted about the stage for many moments, entirely unconscious of a large carving fork stuck into the sawdust which formed the calf of his gladiatorial leg. His look of agony and his roar of anguish—perfect reflections of Forrest's voice and action—when his attention was called to his physical suffering made one of the most ludicrous scenes in the whole history of American burlesque.*

But Brougham went beyond visual comedy; he was a master of language, too. As a critic writing in *Harper's Magazine* in 1895 said, "Until the fall of the curtain, the scintillations of wit and the thunder of puns were incessant and startling."

The following exchange may give you some idea:

"May I ask in the word lie,
What vowel do you use, sir,
I *or* Y?"
*"Y, sir, or I, sir, search the vowels through
And find the one most consonant to you."*

Later the King cries:

*"Sergeant-at-arms, say, what alarms the
    crowd?
Loud noise annoys us; why is it allowed?"*

Yes, words were fine, especially in Brougham's plays, but the shape of things to come in burlesque was found not on a printed page—but on a horse. On June 7, 1861, Adah Isaacs Menken, a girl with a beautiful figure, appeared in tights while strapped to a living horse in a play based on Byron's poem, "Mazeppa."

10

The Greek inspiration endured

Adah Menken as "Mazeppa"

That woman in tights
Adah Isaacs Menken revealed
the shape of things to come
in burlesque while strapped to a
horse (*left*). Below, she
clutches a sword and shield for
protection in another role.

Scandal! Preachers piously fulminated against loose women in tights (a contradiction, if you ask me). But Adah had brought something new to burlesque, and it didn't take theatrical promoters long to grasp the idea. Soon there appeared the most notorious burlesque of its time, *The Black Crook*, featuring "the Amazon Parade of legs."

This was almost too much for one of the critics of the day. "All for what?" he wrote. "A display of brilliant costumes, or rather an absence of them; crowds of girls set in array and posturing so as to bring out every turn and play of the limbs. Throughout it was simply a parade of indecency artistically placed upon the stage, with garish lights to quicken the senses and inflame the passions." Sounds to me as if that critic was "quickened" and "inflamed" himself. I can always tell.

The Beggar's Opera, John Brougham, Adah Isaacs Menken, and *The Black Crook* were just prelude. Burlesque in America at the time was just a small offshoot of show business. The girl whom everyone credits with the establishment of burlesque as an American institution was about to arrive. She came from England, and her name was Lydia Thompson. One hundred years later, I want to salute Lydia and her gorgeous, bouncy British Blondes. Without her, I might not be writing this book today, for there would be no story to write.

Villainy is foiled in *The Black Crook*

NIBLO'S GARDEN.

Lessees and Managers...JARRETT & PALMER.

THE BLACK CROOK!

THE CAST.

COUNT WOLFENSTEIN..Mr. HARRY GWINNETTE
RUDOLPHE (a poor Artist)...Mr. E. K. COLLIER
VON PUFFENGRUNTZ, the Count's Steward..................................Mr. J. W. BRUTONE
HERTZOG, surnamed the BLACK CROOK, an Alchemist......(His Original Part)......Mr. C. H. MORTON
(As played by him over 1,200 times, in New York and principal cities of the United States.)
GREPPO, his Servant.....................................(His Original Part)......Mr. GEORGE ATKINS
DRAGONFIN...Mr. WILLIAM MARTIN
ZAMIEL, the Arch-Fiend..Mr. H. PACKARD
WOLFGAR, a Gypsy Ruffian..Mr. K. WILLIAMS
CASPAR, a Peasant...Mr. J. REA
RED GLARE, the Recording Demon..Mr. W. CARPENTER
SKULDAWELP, familiar to Hertzog...Mr. JULIAN MITCHELL
Villagers, Peasants, Guards, Attendants, Demons, Monsters, Apparitions, Gnomes, &c.
STALACTA, Queen of the Golden Realm.....................................Miss PAULINE MARKHAM
AMINA, betrothed to Rudolphe..Miss LIZZIE KELSEY
DAME BARBARA, her Foster-Mother...Mrs. EDWARD WRIGHT
CARLINE, Amina's Maid...Miss BESSIE SUDLOW
ROSETTA, a Peasant..Miss ADDIE PEARSON

Fairies, Naiads, &c. &c.

The Scene is laid in and around the Hartz Mountains.   A lapse of six months between the 2d and 3d, and 3d and 4th Acts.

ACT FIRST.

Scene I—A Valley at the foot of the Hartz Mountains..........VOEGTLIN
Scene II—A Woody Pass....................................VOEGTLIN
Scene III—Laboratory of the Black Crook..................VOEGTLIN

Scene IV—An Apartment in the Castle of Wolfenstein..........VOEGTLIN
SONG—The Political Whip................................CARLINE.
Scene V—A Wild Glen in the heart of the Brocken.............VOEGTLIN.

GRAND INCANTATION SCENE.
VOEGTLIN.
In this Weird and Thrilling Picture will be presented a series of Novel and Startling Effects.
MARTIN'S MECHANICAL HEAD,   THE FLIGHT OF THE IMPS.   THE CLIMBING SKELETON, &c., &c.

ACT SECOND.

Scene I—Subterranean Vault in the Castle of Wolfenstein......VOEGTLIN
Scene II—Lobby in the Castle of Wolfenstein.................VOEGTLIN
Scene III—A Wild Pass in the Hartz Mountains...............VOEGTLIN

Scene IV—THE GROTTO OF STALACTA............................VOEGTLIN
SONG—Dare I Tell.......................................STALACTA
SONG—Kissing...STALACTA
QUARTETTE...............................STALACTA, CARLINE, RUDOLPHE and GREPPO.

GRAND BALLET!

THE REVEL OF THE SIRENS!!
Invented and arranged by M. IMRE KIRALFY, Maitre de Ballet.
Mlle. ADELE BONI, from LA SCALA, Milan.   Mlle. EMILIA GIAVASSI, from GRAND THEATRE, Florence.
Leontine, Caroline, Marie, Bertha, Gabrielle, Lizette, Dark, Elise, Emily, Jeannette, Strudel, Theresa, Hunt, Joanna, Barotta,
Badoni, Bochanna; and the Entire Corps de Ballet.
THE BATH OF THE SPRITES—THE FOUNTAIN OF JEWELS.

ACT THIRD.

ILLUMINATED GOLDEN TERRACE,...VOEGTLIN
GRAND BALLET OF ALL NATIONS,
Invented and arranged by M. IMRE KIRALFY.
DANCE DE BRETAGNE...CORPS DE BALLET

Entree, PERSIA and RUSSIA..........................CORYPHEES
Entree, SPAIN.....................................DANSEUSES SECONDA
GREAT HUNGARIAN DANCE, Ladies of the KIRALFY TROUPE
MAGYAR VIGADO, (Hungarian Sensational Pas de Cinque,)
Mlle. MANIOLA, EMILIE, KATI KIRALFY;
Mons. IMRE and BOLOSSY KIRALFY.

LA NORMANDIE......................................Mlle GIAVASSI
DANCE SOUTH AMERICAN.....Mm. MARTIN, ARNOLD KIRALFY
and Assistants.
UNITED STATES.....................................Mlle BONI
MAGYAR SOLOS and FRISKA, KIRALFY FAMILY and TROUPE
GRAND FINALE, CHINA, JAPAN, and NATIONS of the WORLD.

By the PREMIERES, SECONDAS, CORYPHEES, CORPS DE BALLET and ONE HUNDRED AND TWENTY AUXILIARIES.
THE LONDON MADRIGAL BOYS WILL SING "SPRING, GENTLE SPRING."
The TWIN SISTERS VERDAY, the most remarkable Child Gymnasts ever known:
M. FELIX REGAMEY, the Great Caricaturist,
In his remarkable entertainment, presenting INSTANTANEOUS GROTESQUE Portraits of Well-known Citizens.
E. D. DAVIES,.....................PREMIER VENTRILOQUIST OF THE WORLD,.............Introducing his New Puppets.

The March of the Amazons.--The Combat!

ACT FOURTH
Terminates with Mr. MATT MORGAN'S

GRAND ALLEGORICAL PICTURES!

1—WINE!   3—WOMEN!   5—FORTUNE IN WAR!
2—WEALTH!   4—POWER!
Closing with the expressive Tableaux
IMMORTALITY!

Stage Manager..............L. J. VINCENT
Musical Conductor..........M. CONNELLY
Stage Machinist............JOHN LEO

Scenic Artist..............W. VOEGTLIN
Properties.................W. DEVERNA
Illuminations..............J. WEATHERSPOON

MATINEES, WEDNESDAY AND SATURDAY.

TREASURER   J. A. ZIMMERMAN.

Pauline Markham, of *The Black Crook*

Backstage burlesque scene, circa 1869

Tintypes of an era
Early chorus girls wore
tights, pantaloons, and very,
very demure expressions.

18

Here come the British Blondes!

WEEKS BEFORE LYDIA THOMPSON'S ARrival, the anticipation was building. She would be the first English actress in history to bring to the United States an entire company of her own. And what a company: beautiful, flirtatious blondes who revealed everything you could reveal within the framework of tights; a battery of young blondes, staring eagerly across the footlights, acting in lusty plays in which sex was the theme. Whoopee! Americans—especially those with bald heads—could hardly wait.

And they were not without help in the anticipation department. In fact, they were teased to death. Lydia's press agent worked overtime in England sending out releases which were printed in American journals as gospel truth. Here is an account of her reception in Europe:

At Helsingfors her pathway was strewn with flowers and the streets illuminated with torches carried by her ardent admirers. At Cologne, the students insisted on sending the horses about their business and drawing the carriage that contained the object of their devotions themselves. At Riga and other Russian towns it became almost a universal custom to exhibit her portrait on one side of the stove to correspond with that of the Czar on the other side. At Lember, a Captain Ludoc Baumbarten of the Russian dragoons, took some flowers and a glove belonging to Miss Thompson, placed them on his breast; then shot himself through the heart, leaving on his table a note stating that his love for her brought on the fatal act.

New York was deluged with pictures of seductive Lydia. In those days, pinups were in the form of cigarette card reproductions, and every jolly bartender had them tacked up around the saloon mirrors. Some showed her in tights; others in short pants or a white dress with a tall painted white hat and umbrella.

Lydia had become famous in London after a spectacular duel in which the weapons were dancing shoes. The story goes that a Spanish beauty named Perea Nina was creating a sensation in London, performing Latin dances. In the press, Miss Nina was wise enough to stir up even more interest by announcing that no English girl could master the intricate technique of the Latin dance.

Lydia Thompson, at that time a relatively unknown actress, challenged Perea to a duel on stage. Lydia won, matching and outmatching her Latin rival's every step and pirouette. The English press was ecstatic.

Showing a true Englishwoman's spirit, she vindicated the honor of her country while demonstrating perfection in a type of dancing heretofore deemed impossible for an English artiste to acquire.

Lydia became the idol of the Empire—and the ever-present promoters moved in. Samuel Colville, an American manager, and Alexander Henderson, who was also Lydia's husband, decided to assemble a troupe called the "British Blondes" with Lydia as the star, and company manager. The Blondes included some other noted beauties of the English stage: Pauline Markham of the Queen's Theatre; Lisa Weber of Covent Garden; and Ada Harland of the Strand Theatre.

The long-awaited engagement of Lydia Thompson and the British Blondes precipitated a barrage of criticism—and long, long lines at the box office. The year was 1869. Wood's Theatre, which would be the location of the heralded debut, was renovated at a cost of thirty thousand dollars. *Ixion, Ex-King of Thessaly* by F. C. Burand was the opening attraction. One historian says that it was a "dull, juvenile story about miscellaneous mortals and jumbled mythology." But it sounds pretty lively to me.

The ex-King Ixion, played by shapely Lydia, is invited to Mount Olympus where he meets among others, Juno, Venus, Neptune, the Three Graces, the Nine Muses—and sundry English and French sailors. What were sailors doing on Mt. Olympus? Why did Lydia play a man's role and look shapely? Who knows.

But the show must have been fun, because it was an immediate hit—and it ran in New York and around the country for ten years. Even the critics, in trying to blast the show, made it sound inviting. Here are some of the unfriendly reviews:

It is impossible to give an idea of this sustained burlesque. It resembles an Irish stew as one minute they are dancing a cancan and the next singing a psalm tune. It is a bewilderment of limbs, bella donna, and grease paint.

And another:

To represent Minerva with a fan and whiskey flask, Jupiter as a jig dancer, Venus with a taste for the cancan, is all done, we suppose, in a laudable spirit of burlesque, but we could almost hate Miss Thompson and her assistants for spoiling this pretty story.

On the prudery front, one writer took dead aim at the lively eyes of the blondes:

That a large number of actresses are virtuous, does not prevent vice from flourishing to an alarming extent in "the profession," and this being the case, how can one wonder at a number of girls regarding the stage as a means of arriving at infamous luxury, and endeavoring to attract the notice of those who are in a position to gratify their aspirations, by displaying their beauties to the utmost advantage?

Later on in this same review, the author gives his impression of the audience. Quite an impression! It reveals the possible origin of the bald-head row of my day.

When one regards the rows of bald heads, palsied jaws, pendulous cheeks and bleared eyes in the stalls, and the raffish blackguardism in the rest of the house, one is inclined to dispute the use of the word "public."

Blonde trailblazer
Lydia Thompson brought her British Blondes to New York, and made burlesque an American institution.

What did the Blondes have that drew the men with pendulous cheeks and bleared eyes? They looked like advertisements for a diet drink. In those days men preferred their beauties to be voluptuous, a tradition going back to the Italian Renaissance. It was a tradition that did not die easily. Years later, a touring burlesque show was still advertising for chorus girls, and specifying that no girl under 150 pounds need apply. Whether you think they were voluptuous—or just plump—the Blondes had pazazz. No

Amelia Summerville

Molly Fuller

Anne Sutherland

doubt about it. And the lady with the most was, unquestionably, the redoubtable Lydia. Here is Lydia in her prime, the way one reporter saw her:

Lydia Thompson is simply irresistible. She is very brilliant in appearance, and full of piquancy. Brightness in everything is the term which best describes her style. Whether talking, singing, dancing, or indulging in grotesquerie, she is always fascinating.

Elsewhere in the review, the reporter alluded to the success of the show.

The British Blondes' career is too well known to require more than a passing word. They opened in New York and made a success almost unparalleled in the dramatic history of the city, having appeared for forty-five consecutive weeks to overflowing houses. For the three final nights of their stay at Niblo's Garden, the receipts amounted to nearly $6,000.

Their tour throughout the country has likewise been one continued triumph. They have attracted crowded audiences in every city in which they have appeared. In Chicago the rank and fashion of the city attended their performances, and all endorsed the opinion formed elsewhere of the individual talent and collective completeness of the troupe.

Lydia Thompson and her British Blondes toured this country to such acclaim for ten years. In doing so, she made burlesque an American institution, known and loved in every city in the land. It wasn't until World War II's Lend Lease program that we repaid this debt to the British. And even then, President Roosevelt didn't acknowledge it. If no one minds, I'll do it for him.

Pauline Markham reclines on a tiger skin

NINA FARRINGTON

IRENE VERONA

ROSE HAMILTON

ANNA MANTELL

USE LITTLE RHODY CUT PLUG.

USE LITTLE RHODY CUT PLUG.

USE LITTLE RHODY CUT PLUG.

In chewing tobacco, a plug for each pretty girl

Some honest femininity with the same kind of cut

"Judge for yourselves, boys."

Mignon

Minolo

Mona

Nanette

Nina

Bella

Pearl

Rosita

Stephanie

Teresa

Ima

BALLET QUEENS
Given with each box of
Wm. S. Kimball & Co's
CIGARETTES
Mademoiselles

JULETTE	FLORENCE
CONSUELO	FLORA
IDA	FAVORITA
FLORETTE	FAVETTE
MIGNON	GABRIELLE
PEARL	HORTENSE
EDITA	HENRIETTE
BETTINA	IMRY
ANNETTE	IMOGENE
ARVITA	IRENE
ALMA	LAURETTE
BELLA	LAURENCE
COZETTE	MINOLO
CORINNE	MUZETTE
CORINTH	MONA
CELIA	NINA
DONNA	NANETTE
DORA	NUMA
EFFIE	OCTAVIA
ELVINA	OLGA
ESTELLE	PETITA
ETTA	FLORINE
ELFINA	ROSITA
FANTINE	STEPHANIE
CROIZETTE	TERESA

Cigarette cards with pretty people

Playing cards doubled as pin-ups

Venus in a body stocking. Shocking!

Mr. Weber, meet Mr. Fields

IN THE LATE 1800S, A MAN NAMED MIchael B. Leavitt revolutionized burlesque. For centuries, burlesque had been presented as plays, or farces. Leavitt created a burlesque show. The opening he borrowed from the minstrel show, cleverly replacing the endmen with girls. The "olio" consisting of vaudeville acts was the second act. The grand finale was a burlesque farce in the classic tradition.

Leavitt billed his first show as *Mme. Rentz's Female Minstrels*, and his star was one of the greatest soubrettes ever to be associated with burlesque. Stories are told of gentlemen admirers engaging in fist fights and tumbling onto the stage while Mabel Rentz was doing her act. She must have been the very mistress of suggestion, for in those days the sight of a bare ankle was all that was allowed. A fellow actor named John Henshaw described one of Mabel's triumphs:

We had advertised that we were going to put on the cancan. Mabel did this number and when the music came to the dum-de-dum she raised her foot just about twelve inches, whereupon the entire audience hollered, "Whooo!" It set them crazy. Yes. Just that little gesture—the slight suggestion. It became the talk of the town.

Burlesque shows were now springing up in all quarters, and poor Mr. Leavitt soon had a dozen rival companies on the road. One of these was the Ada Richmond Burlesquers, and today it is remembered in burlesque history only because of two comedians who started in show business with the troupe. Their names: Lew Weber and Joe Fields.

They were not the first of the straight man–comic teams but they almost instantly became the most famous. They were forerunners of generation after generation of two-man comedy teams, from Gallagher and Shean, to Abbott and Costello, to Martin and Lewis, to the Smothers Brothers.

As I write these words I remember my friend, the late A. J. Liebling, one of the finest journalists America has ever produced, and one of the greatest burlesque buffs. He and his wife used to come to our show time after time—and afterwards Joe Liebling would delight in cornering our comics and straight men in the Reno Bar—the Lower East Side Sardi's—and asking them to describe their techniques.

Joe couldn't get over Connie Ryan, our straight man at the time. Indeed, Connie could have posed for a pattern of all straight men who ever played burlesque. He was sharply dressed, a flower in his button-hole (always useful for gags), his hair slicked back, shoes pointed—in Joe Liebling's words, "He must kill them in

Impresario Michael Leavitt

The immortal cancan
France influenced burlesque
with the cancan dance.
For a glimpse of a lady's
ankle, San Francisco miners
(below) would pay gold.

Dayton." The classic straight man was just that: a Main Street sharpie with the girls at his feet.

But you had to have talent to be a great straight man. You didn't just stand there and read cue-lines for the comic to deliver his jokes. As Connie explained to Liebling, "A straight man doesn't just set up gags; he has a role to play. He must attack the comedian, scold him, batter him down, make him fight back.

That's when the comic is funny—and that's when the audience is pulling for the comic to outwit the overbearing straight man."

Connie Ryan and Steve Mills were latter-day descendants of Weber and Fields, the original burlesque comedy team. Lew Fields, the straight man, was tall, almost handsome. Joe Weber was short and furtive-looking. They both wore spade beards, and sported derby

Great comedy pair
Weber and Fields were the most famous comedy team of their day. They sang sentimental songs, told dialect stories, did acrobatics, and acted out parodies and burlesques. Their names became household words, and in innumerable roles they dominated the U.S. stage for years.

hats. They could do nearly anything on stage. If an Irish act was wanted, they'd open the act singing, "Here we are, an Irish pair." If German, "Here we are, a German pair." They improvised, sang sentimental songs, performed acrobatic tumbling, told dialect stories, acted out parodies and burlesques—and everything they did was served up with a generous portion of roustabout slapstick.

Dutch dialect acts have disappeared in this country today; nobody does them. But around the turn of the century, almost every burlesque show had a Dutch act. Weber and Fields did one of the best. A sample of the dialect will give you an idea:

LEW: *"If you luf her, vy don't you send her some poultry?"*
JOE: *"She don't need no poultry; her father is a butcher."*
LEW: *"I mean luf voids like Romeo and Chuliet talks:*
If you luf me like I luf me
No knife can cut us togedder."

It is Weber and Fields, too, who created the single most quoted joke in all American history:

"Who was that lady I saw you with last night?"
"That was no lady, that was my wife!"

Weber and Fields eventually outgrew burlesque and started a famous vaudeville theatre in New York. They remain one of the immortal teams in American comedy, and their memory still lingers in burlesque whenever a straight man throws a zinger in to the comic.

Weber and Fields played the East Coast, but burlesque was moving all over America. In those days, a traveling company ran into obstacles that today's travelers wouldn't dream of—including drunken cowboys, renegade Indians, and shoot-'em-ups right in the theatre.

In his fine book, *Burleycue: An Underground History of Burlesque*, published in 1932, burlesque historian Bernard Sobel recorded interviews of some of the burlesque stars who toured the wild, wild West in the late 1800s. Apparently, it was no picnic, as a delightful girl named Annie Ashley reported after an engagement in Tombstone, Arizona. The trouble in Tombstone was a feud, involving the famous Earp brothers. As Annie's show was the "only wheel in town" the feudists attended. In Annie's words:

Earning money then was exciting, to say the least. Every night the feudists would come to the theatre; sometimes meet each other, and shoot it out then and there. The boxes were built in a ring like a horseshoe, and one gang would sit on one side and the other opposite. Once our blackface comedian, Billy Hart, was on the stage when a cowboy came in and shot the wig off his head—just for devilment.

As soon as trouble started everyone used to drop down and lie flat on his face—everybody. If we were dancing, and the shooting commenced, the lights would go out and we'd lie down flat on our stomachs for protection.

As fickle as a barometer was the change in conditions. One morning the feud would be on, then a dead quiet would ensue—a quiet intended to deceive the enemy. Suddenly another feud was on. It was between the famous Earp brothers, who were the marshals, Curly Bill, a Mexican, and Frank Stillwell, a nice quiet man, though an outlaw. One night something serious happened. Morgan Earp was killed while in the Green Chop House by a shot which came in through the window while he was playing billiards. That renewed the battle. For a few hours everything was quiet—an ominous quiet—a silence intended to cheat the enemy into believing that everything was all right again. But the Earp brothers were out to avenge Morgan's death and the next day sixteen men lay strewn on the sidewalk, sprawled out in their own blood—dead. Everyone could see them lying right there. Then they got and killed Frank Stillwell and Curly Bill out on a prairie somewhere between Tombstone and Dunning.

Miss Ashley sums up demurely:
This happened while we were playing there—a singular experience for a young girl to pass through.

Annie Ashley was just one of the burlesque queens of the gay eighties and nineties. There was Ida Siddons who

"The higher the skirt, the greater the crowd"

whirled her way through a rope and fire dance; Louise Montague, "The $10,000 Beauty" (in those days, a dollar was a dollar), and most famous of all, Little Egypt, who introduced the belly dance to this country.

Little Egypt never saw the Nile, but she could have taught Cleopatra a few tricks. It's said that, when she went into her act, traffic stopped outside in fear of an earthquake.

Belly dancing involves the most vigorous rotation of the hips that any young lady can possibly execute. It is performed in two major phases: *cifitelli*, slow sensual convolutions; and *karsilama*, joyous, fast whirlings. As the tempo increases to *karsilama*, the audience usually begins to clap rhythmically, spurring the belly dancer on to faster and faster undulations.

Little Egypt probably knew none of these terms and definitions—*karsilama* to her would have been a mystery. No matter. She certainly knew how to rotate those hips. She opened at Sam T. Jack's burlesque theatre with the act, but really hit her stride at the Columbia Exposition in 1904. Americans had never seen this sinuous, erotic dance before—with its hints of the forbidden world of harems, and fat sheiks lolling around with tender, young girls.

Little Egypt really started something. Soon, almost every burlesque show had a belly dancer from the chorus, who would stop the show in an "Oriental" number. For some long-forgotten reason, these dancers were called cooch dancers.

The century ended; men looked forward to a new and brighter one hundred years. What marvels would the new century bring? For burlesque, the marvels came fast. In the very first two decades, it entered into its Golden Age. The greatest comics this nation has ever seen were about to step onto its tawdry stage and light it with a blaze that still flourishes. In 1900 the world of burlesque might have said, as Al Jolson proclaimed years later: "You ain't seen nuthin' yet!"

Miss Montague

Miss Santley

Mabel Santley created a sensation with her cancan. Louise Montague was "The $10,000 Beauty."

The opulent Sadie Leonard

Far from Cairo
Little Egypt originated
the American version
of the belly dance,
known in those days (1905)
as the hootchy-kootchy.

The golden era of burlesque

Eddie Cantor, in blackface

BURLESQUE WAS LIKE A ROCKET THAT GOT off the ground in 1900 when Sam Scribner formed the Columbia Circuit. Along the way there were some of the brightest sparks ever seen in show business—sparks that issued forth from a group of comedians whose names read like a roll call of a Hall of Fame of humor. Among them were W. C. Fields, Will Rogers, Bert Lahr, Ed Wynn, Joe E. Brown, Leon Errol, Buster Keaton, Joe Penner, Eddie Cantor, Bobby Clark, Al Jolson, Jimmy Durante, and Abbott and Costello.

Burlesque was the breeding grounds for these great comics. It gave them a stage, an audience, and a chance to develop the acts, mannerisms, pantomime, or whatever made them famous. Al Jolson sang his first song in a burlesque house. Joe E. Brown was part of an acrobatic team; he had never said a word on stage or tried to be funny until he entered burlesque.

It was like the minor leagues of theatre for comics—and where do we have that today? Nowhere. That's one of the great tragedies of modern show business. If a comic talent comes along today, where does he develop his act? He won't be booked into a theatre on stage, you can bet that. He won't be placed on a television show, if he's had no experience; the costs are too high.

They can't afford it. So what does he do? Chances are he finds a tiny nightclub with a desperate owner and tries out a monologue on a few friends who show up for support. But a monologue isn't the whole business of comedy. Charlie Chaplin, who got his start in English Music Halls, the English equivalent of burlesque, never delivered a monologue in his life.

I read one recently published book about burlesque, written by a gentleman who didn't like it. This author was a peculiar fellow because he wrote a book whose whole theme seemed to be how much he disliked burlesque, how overrated its comedy was, and so on and so forth. Unfortunately for his integrity, he also revealed that he'd seen about two hundred burlesque shows in his life. I think he hated it so much he loved it.

What really upset me about this book was that the writer tried to play down the importance of burlesque as a training ground for the great comics I've mentioned. He said that they appeared just "briefly" in burlesque and almost immediately went on to "better" things—and that burlesque fans had built up a phony legend about its role in developing these talents.

Well, I could quote numerous historians to prove him completely wrong, but the greatest authorities are the comics themselves. A few years ago Danny Thomas went on television and opened his show by informing the nationwide audience that he had started his career in burlesque and learned most of what he knows about comedy right there. There were many in the studio audience who couldn't believe that the star of the Danny Thomas Family show would even admit that he had been in burlesque, let alone that he owed his skill to it.

Unfortunately, even today—and perhaps I, myself, am part of the reason for it—most of the people who have never seen a burlesque show are convinced that it's strictly a striptease marathon, and the comics just fill in the pauses while the strippers—and the audience—catch their breath. W. C. Fields, a filler? Bert Lahr? Eddie Cantor? And in the modern day, Jackie Gleason? Red Skelton? Danny Thomas?

I'd like to quote a wonderful man, the late Joe E. Brown, to put the real story into perspective. In his autobiography, Brown wrote:

The public's low opinion of burlesque today has caused more than one prominent star to soft-pedal his (or her) humble beginnings in the field. I am much too grateful for the things I learned in burlesque to belittle its importance in my story. It was a fortunate thing for me that Frank Prevost decided burlesque would be a good place to try my comedy. It was a fortunate thing for me that he recognized comedy talents in me.

Joe E. Brown had been an acrobat in a team, traveling in circuses. He was athletic (his love of baseball became an American legend) but no one thought to give his comedy talents a try. Prevost was Brown's acrobatic partner, and he saw the comic genius in Brown that no one else had noticed. Together they worked up a comedy routine, and Prevost managed to book the act with a burlesque show called *The Ideals*. Salary: $60 a week for the two of them. They opened in Minneapolis. Their performance was a surprise hit. Prevost came out in his full dress and opera hat, looking very much the well-dressed man-about-town. Brown followed him in the same clothes—but something was wrong. The suit hung slightly askew.

Prevost took off his collapsible hat, carefully folded it, and tucked it under his arm. Brown took off his silk hat and crushed it under his arm as though it were a paper bag. Prevost pulled off his gloves, neatly folded them, and put them in his inside breast pocket. Brown began to take off his gloves—and disaster! He couldn't get them off. They were too long! Brown had asked his landlady to sew several lengths of her stockings to the cuffs. Finally, he got them off, painfully, wadded them up, and stuck them inside his coat. Meanwhile, they went into their acrobatic act, and Brown imitated everything Prevost did with that same kind of buffoonery. And Brown heard for the first time the sound that would engulf him on stage his whole life: laughter.

They laughed. I kept saying that over and over to myself. It was one of the great highlights of my life. To hear people laugh, to think that they were laughing at something I did! . . . I thought, maybe I can do other things, things I haven't even rehearsed, things I haven't even thought of.

Now we see just exactly how burlesque aided a comic in development. For this act of Brown's was pure pantomime—even his partner, Prevost, never suggested that he *say* anything. The buffoonery was merely a gimmick to make their acrobatic act funnier. And then one day, purely by accident, it happened. As Brown tells the story:

We said nothing during our act at this time, and it was not until weeks later that I uttered any sound. I realized one day that one particularly difficult trick was greatly appreciated by the audience, so I practiced doing it with a great show of ease. Bouncing from a bounding mat or trampoline, I would do a double back somersault and body twist and land standing on Prevost's shoulders. I'd grin and look at the audience as though it were as easy as pie. One day, in a high squeaky voice, I said, "Did you see that?"

It brought the house down—and Joe E. Brown became a comedian in the full sense. From then on he wasn't just an acrobat who did funny tricks. He was a comedian, who happened to do acrobatics, and then, eventually, a full-fledged comedian. Joe E. Brown was in burlesque for eleven years. He played nearly every burlesque house in the country, in shows such as the *Moulin Rouge Burlesquers* and *Uncle Sam's Belles*. All this time he was developing and polishing his act, becoming an established comedian.

Occasionally he was also sparring with John L. Sullivan, whose act was a feature of many burlesque shows. After the sparring sessions, John L. would usually ask Joe E. to join him in a dinner of "pig's ass and cabbage." Joe E. always found some excuse.

In 1918 Brown's burlesque show was appearing in New York at the Columbia Theatre, and Henry Cort, the son of the famous producer, John Cort, caught his act. He came backstage and offered Joe E. a part in a Broadway show, *Listen, Lester*. Brown accepted, the play was a hit, and a new world opened for the fabulous Joe E. Brown. But he never forgot where he learned his trade.

W.C. Fields is another great comedian who started as a trick artist—in this

case, a juggler—and then became a comedian. Never has there been anyone like W. C. Fields. Years after his death, he's still an idol. Top comedians imitate his nasal twang; teen-agers collect big pop-art posters, some of them full-length, showing the pugnacious oldster with the red, bulbous nose. And television never seems to stop running his pictures on the late show.

Why not? This man wasn't just a comic. He was a genius, called by some the greatest comic of all time. I don't know about that, I've seen and known too many great comics to make a choice—but I do know he was funny, in a very special way.

This was the man who strolled into an elegant hotel one day, all alone, and asked the surprised desk clerk for the bridal suite. The clerk icily informed Fields that the bridal suite was reserved only for gentlemen with brides.

"That's OK," intoned Fields. "I'll pick one up in town."

In his later years, Fields liked to recall that his first job was as a professional "drowner." He was a young boy from Philadelphia with a juggling technique already well advanced after weeks of painful practice. For ten dollars a week he was hired to juggle on Fortescue's Pier in Atlantic City. Unfortunately, few

people came to see him juggle—or to see any other of the Fortescue acts. But the company manager was resourceful. At periodic intervals during the day, he would send Fields out into the ocean over his head, where Fields would proceed to thrash around and cry out for help. A Fortescue lifeguard would rush out and drag the drowning swimmer to the safety of the pier. By then a crowd would have gathered, and the rest was up to the barker. Believe it or not, Fields did this every few hours, swimming out into the water, flailing around, and gulping gallons of salt water accidentally, only to be dragged in like a drowned rat.

Years later, while nursing a tumbler of Scotch, he would explain his fondness for alcohol. "If you drowned twelve times a day for six weeks, you'd never drink water again, either." Smiling, he would pour the whiskey down his throat.

Fields was going exactly nowhere in Atlantic City, unless it was to a watery death, and then one of those ubiquitous burlesque company managers, always on the lookout for promising—and cheap—talent, hired him for a traveling show. The show traveled only as far as Kent, Ohio, where the manager departed, stranding the company. But Fields soon caught on with another burlesque show, Fulton's, and when that

Comic juggler
W.C. Fields began his career (*right*) as a juggler of everything from hats to mice. He was cantankerous, rude, obnoxious—and people loved him. Below, he accepts a cigar.

closed, moved in with an even better show, Fred Irwin's. In these months he developed the act which was to make him famous. He juggled everything—cigars, white mice, bananas—and during the juggling he kept up a running monologue. As Fields later told a reporter:

You see, although my specialty was juggling, I used it only as a means to an end. I didn't just stand up and toss balls, knives, plates, and clubs. I invented little acts, which would seem like episodes out of real life.

Somehow, even though I was only a kid, I had sense enough to know that I must work my mind and not just my hands. If I hadn't realized that, I'd be laid on the shelf today. People would be saying, "Bill Fields? Oh yes, he used to be a juggler, didn't he?"

Fred Irwin's burlesque show was of the old-time variety; that is, it consisted of one-act plays, with Fields's routine as a filler. Occasionally, Fields would play some of the comic roles when one or another of the regular comedians was ill, indisposed, or drunk. One occasion he remembered, with typical Fields relish, took place in Columbus, Ohio. He had to substitute in the role of a dastardly saw-mill operator in a melodrama. The climax of this act occurred when a very shapely ingenue, strapped on a conveyor belt, moved helplessly toward the sharp-toothed saw, operated by the villain, Fields.

It so happened that this beautiful ingenue had made a terrible mistake, under the circumstances. She had been resisting Fields's romantic advances all during the tour. Now, here she was, strapped hand and foot to a conveyor belt, moving like a slice of pie to the cutter. And the cutter was the guy she had insulted just last night! Don't panic, the girl must have thought. Fields won't do anything dumb in front of all these people.

Then, moving inexorably on the belt towards the villain, she saw a horrible sight: Fields's *smile*. In a flash, she knew. Fields was going to make her pay for those midnight refusals. She screamed. Oh my, did she scream. And the audience roared. This girl was a real actress, they thought. And wasn't it clever how that saw-mill operator seemed to be actually cutting the girl into slabs.

Fields never touched her—but only a juggler could have guided that saw to a thousandth of an inch from her quivering tummy. "One of my most superb performances," Fields recalled later, in one of his expansive moods. "From then on, ingenues treated me with respect and fear, which is as good as love, and usually ends up in the same place."

Wherever the burlesque show traveled,

Fields was getting rave notices, such as this one in the Denver *Post:*

Fields was a knockout last night, a comic who reaches the heights of juggling perfection . . . it is said that the engagement of three days will be all too short for everybody to see this consummate artist.

And in due time, the managers of vaudeville came to his dressing room, to offer him the chance to rise from burlesque into the big time. No doubt they were feeling magnanimous—and patronizing. But they didn't know Fields.

He stunned them by saying he might consent to join vaudeville, but only under the proper billing. And that should read very clearly in big, black print: "W. C. FIELDS, THE DISTINGUISHED COMEDIAN."

When the vaudeville impresarios recovered from shock, they reminded Fields that he was known as a juggler, not a comedian. Besides, he damn well wasn't distinguished. But Fields had his way. He got his billing, and he more than lived up to it, as the whole world knows. He *was* a distinguished comedian. Today everyone delights in remembering the old rogue who, when he saw a darling puppy, kicked it in the teeth. They loved the man who, when engaged to make a movie with darling Baby Leroy, put Scotch in his milk bottle. Baby Leroy took one swig and got pie-eyed; he

couldn't go on with the scene. Fields was disgusted: "The kid ain't no trooper!"

I wish I had time and space in this book to pay tribute at length to all of those great comedians who came from what *Variety* once called "the great cradle of talent." But these must be mentioned, for I'm proud of them all.

Al Jolson, for example, one of the greatest entertainers of all time—a man who could both sing and make people laugh—started out in show business as a boy selling water for one cent a glass in the balcony of a burlesque theatre in Washington. One day they gave him a chance to sing. A boy of fifteen, he stood in the aisle, while on stage two girls with the delightful names of Celeste and Beleste joined him in a trio. The producer of that show, Al Reeves, recalled years later, "He would tie up the show. He was a riot from the first. Everything would be perfectly *still* as he sang."

Leon Errol, who was to perform so unforgettably in the *Ziegfeld Follies*, not only appeared in burlesque, he staged his own shows. A historian of the time recalls one of his most popular acts. He plays a drunk who staggers by accident into a dancing class. The girls think he is their dance instructor. So as he staggers, and swoops, and stumbles about the room, the surprised girls duplicate

The "Singing Fool"
Al Jolson is shown on stage and in his dressing room at the Winter Garden. Al's slogan was: "You ain't seen nuthin yet."

Errol's perils
Leon Errol delighted fans
with his "tipsy" act. Whether
snuggling up to a girl with
a glass of champagne, or
going it alone—he was great.

his every move. It was not only funny,
it was a ballet of astonishing precision.
With twenty girls falling to the floor, ris-
ing, only to stagger again, collapse, or
follow whatever their drunken "instructor" was doing, it's said the audience itself ended up on the floor doubled over
almost in pain at the fun.

Eddie Cantor, later the pop-eyed darling of the screen and radio, didn't exactly begin like W. C. Fields as a juggler.

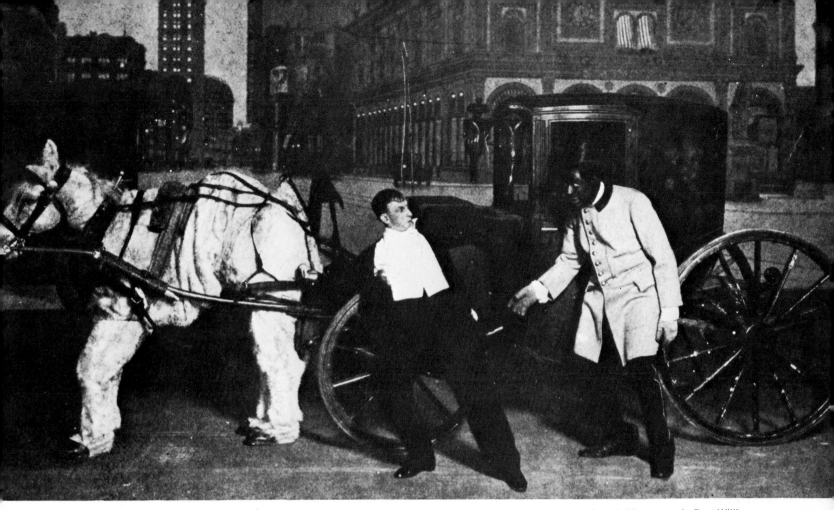

Leon confounds Negro comic Bert Williams

He began as a juggler's assistant, in a burlesque show called *Apple of Paris*.

His job was to pick up the pieces of missed plates, etc., in a comedy act. Then one day, Eddie made a funny remark about one of the missed plates as he picked it up—and the audience laughed. From then on he started pushing the managers for a job of his own—and eventually they allowed him to sing. His first song was a now-forgotten Irving Berlin tune, "Mr. Brown Has a Violin." It was such a knockout, the audience roared for an encore, and Eddie gave them another Irving Berlin song which is still a hit, "Alexander's Ragtime Band." I can still see Eddie as we all remember him, clapping those hands and jumping in a rhythm step as he socked his numbers to the audience. He was one of the great ones.

Recently, my friend Bert Lahr passed away, and the newspapers were filled with stories of his celebrated past, none of them failing to mention his years in burlesque.

I knew Bert well, and worked with him for a while when he staged a show called *Burlesque* some years ago. The great thing about Bert was that he never changed as far as his stage personality went. He was one of the fantastic muggers of all time; his large face seemed

Jessel and Cantor, 1918

Love and Kisses
Eddie Cantor

The East Side Kid
Eddie Cantor was one
of many remarkably
talented comedians who
grew up on New York's
Lower East Side.
He appears with boyhood
friend George Jessel
at far left, and
again below in a scene
from *Kid Cabaret*.
At right, Cantor with
Fanny Brice in
the *Ziegfeld Follies*.

almost to be made of rubber, and he could contort it in a thousand funny ways. When Bert came on stage, the audience knew it was in for fun. There was no mistaking the fact. Bert wasn't one of those subtle comedians—he played it strictly for laughs, and the broader the better, and the better the audience liked it. He'd scamper up a wall, slip on a banana peel, leer at a pretty girl—and the audience would be convulsed.

The strange thing is, Bert Lahr was one of the most conservative men off stage I ever met in show business. Meeting him and his lovely family in a restaurant you would be sure he was a slightly weary Wall Street lawyer, after a hard day of corporate maneuvering. Then, the next day you'd see him on stage, baggy pants and ripped shirt, roaring and carrying on in great style.

Bobby Clark and his painted eyeglasses will never be forgotten, either. He was all burlesque, and no bones about it. He started in burlesque with a partner, Paul McCullough, and the team of Clark and McCullough soon became one of the most famous in show business. Bobby loved props, and he used them all the time. He'd come on stage with a cigar clenched in his teeth, a cane in his hand, and painted eyeglasses on his face. Why the paint? Why not real eyeglasses? "*These* I can't lose," he'd say.

Florenz Ziegfeld signs up Bert Lahr

The life of the show
Bert Lahr was a top
star in Ziegfeld days
and long afterward.
He endeared himself
to audiences in
countless stage and film
productions, with
a zany slapstick style
born in his burlesque
days. His irrepressible
humor was the comedy
of a master clown.

Lahr as an Apache dancer

Lahr as a matador

A born clown
Bert Lahr's mobile face was like India rubber. He could stretch it eighteen ways for a laugh. In the late forties he came back to Broadway as the star of a play called *Burlesque.* On the opposite page, he is seen as a Yukon gold miner in full cry.

Giants of burlesque
Bobby Clark, always
with painted eyeglasses,
appears at left with
partner Paul McCullough.
At right he does the
famous Courtroom scene
with Gypsy Rose Lee
on radio, years before
Sammy Davis made
"Heah come de judge" a
national call to laughter.

Another comedian who loved props was Ed Wynn. But his props were even more sensational. No one who ever saw his act will forget the corn-on-the-cob typewriter carriage. It would ring a bell when the eater reached the end of the line. When he ate a grapefruit, he wore eyeglasses with windshield wipers. He changed hats constantly during a performance, each one funnier than the previous. Here he had help. His father was in the millinery trade.

Buster Keaton went on from burlesque to the movies, where he became known as "The Great Stone Face." Some modern-day critics, looking back at those movies, now declare he was the greatest comic of them all, with that flat hat and concrete expression which never changed during the most violent comic chases.

Joe Penner went from burlesque to radio to become famous, with his sayings like "Ya Wanna Buy a Duck?"

The Perfect Fool
Ed Wynn was called the Perfect Fool. As a burlesque star, he believed in clownish costumes, props, makeup— anything for a laugh. Years later, he was to delight television audiences as the Texaco Fire Chief, still using the burlesque routines of long ago.

The duck seller
"Wanna Buy a Duck?" was Joe Penner's perennial question, and all America answered yes.

Thirty years later, I can't remember why *that* was funny, but it became one of the most quoted sayings in the land. He also would stop a man on the street and say, "Come to my house for a chicken dinner. You bring the chicken!"

Will Rogers is the only one of the above comics who wasn't in burlesque for a *long* time. But there are playbills extant to prove he *was* in burlesque, with his famous act of trick rope-twirling. He went on to the *Ziegfeld Follies*, and then to the movies, and then to national prominence as a humorous commentator on political and national news.

Only Will Rogers could have written the following letter to *The New York Times*, when that newspaper declared it was not responsible for the views Rogers expressed in his daily column.

Beverly Hills, Calif. Dec. 7
I would like to state to the readers of The New York Times *that I am in no way responsible for the editorial or political policy of this paper.*

The "Schnoz"
Jimmy Durante had a nose that was to make him famous. His raspy voice can still be heard singing "Inka-dinka-doo!"

He never smiled
Buster Keaton was known as "The Great Stone Face." He left burlesque to win movie fame.

I allow them free reign as to their opinion so long as it is within the bounds of good subscription gathering.

But I want it distinctly understood that their policy may be in direct contrast to mine.

Their editorials may be put in purely for humor, or just to fill space.

Every paper must have its various entertaining features, and their editorials are not always to be taken seriously, and never to be construed as my policy.

Yours,
Will Rogers

Don't give our regards to Broadway

IN THE FIRST DECADE OF THE TWENTIETH century, a girl named Anna Held took a bath in milk. It was neither pasteurized nor homogenized, but it was publicized. The brains behind this unusual dairy and sex gimmick was Anna's husband, Florenz Ziegfeld, and those same brains were to spell the temporary doom of burlesque once again.

Anna Held was a demure, little brunette with impish eyes, and she must have been a corker. Because Ziegfeld planned a show for her that would have sent any other star screaming through the window. He would surround little Anna Held with *twelve* tall and gorgeous girls. The show was *The Little Duchess*, a title that could have been applied to Anna herself. Because in the midst of these tall beauties, she still held the attention of the audience. Maybe those milk baths did have something!

Encouraged by this success, Ziegfeld used the identical technique in two new productions, *The Parisian Model*, and *Mlle. Napoleon*. But this time he had a further surprise for the audience: nudity—or, at least, the illusion of it. When the curtains parted for one scene, the audience saw an artist's studio, and six easels. Behind each easel stood a show girl in a long cloak. The easel blocked the important area of each body, a fact which became apparent when the girls threw off their cloaks and the audience saw bare shining shoulders and bare legs.

Were they really nude? Well, they were in an artist's studio, weren't they? And artists painted nude girls, one of the few facts about art that every red-blooded American boy knows.

In actuality, the girls were in strapless evening gowns holding on for dear life to rolled-up hems above their knees. But the scene was a knockout, and Ziegfeld's ideas soared onward and upward.

Why not go all the way with the girl theme? Why not a show with 120 beautiful girls? These girls, as historian Marjorie Farnsworth put it, would have "figures as provocative as their faces; tall, stately girls, radiant with youth and draped in priceless costumes of furs, gems, laces, ribbons and flowers, who would need only to walk with patrician grace before the footlights. He envisioned these beauties dressed to represent the seasons, months, nations of the world, celebrated courtesans of history, grains of the fields, leaves of trees, animals of the jungle, flowers of the garden." And some of them, in tableaus, would be nude.

What else besides girls? Music? A *hundred* musicians. How the musicians' union would love that man today—and how Ziegfeld would hate them! With today's union regulations he would have had to settle for a juke box and a drummer.

Comedy? He would have not one comedian, but six—and the greatest of the world.

On these two fronts, nudity and comedy, he struck a dagger into bosomy burlesque's breast.

Meanwhile, burlesque was going in just the reverse of Ziegfeld. The Columbia Circuit, under the guidance of Sam Scribner, was becoming more and more conservative. Scribner, of all things, was a moralist. He constantly railed against offensive remarks and gestures on stage. He cautioned the theatre operators again and again about showing too much flesh.

In 1907 Ziegfeld unveiled his first *Follies*, an immediate smash hit which was to be repeated year after year in new editions. Earl Carroll also got into the act with his *Vanities*. And that meant Broadway had at least two shows running every year with more nudity than the supposedly scandalous burlesque.

In terror the burlesque operators went to Scribner. They complained that Earl Carroll's revue was showing bare breasts. Couldn't they show at least one bare breast? Scribner said, "No," and, while he was at it, warned his theatrical producers not to allow the expressions "hell," "damn," "God," "cock-eyed liar," "son-of-a-gun," and "son-of-a-Polack." As an *American Mercury* writer put it in 1924, "Pretty soon there'll be nothing left for people who want to enjoy a good old-fashioned rough-house evening save the high-priced Broadway revues."

Naughtiness was not the only thing that scuttled burlesque at that period. Ziegfeld was a strange man, strange because he is said to have had no sense of humor. And yet, he personally scouted burlesque shows in search of burlesque comedy talent. He came up with the winners every time.

Leon Errol opened in his first revue and played in almost every other edition. Leon, the classic rubbery-legged drunk, played in scenes with W. C. Fields that must have been classics of alcohol content as well as humor.

Fields became a Ziegfeld steady, appearing in many editions. He must have been a wild one to work with. There is a legendary story about his days in the *Follies* in which a midget or Ed Wynn—take your choice—crouched beneath his billiard table while he was doing his famous billiard scene with the crooked cue. Wynn—or the midget— would mug at the audience while Fields

Ziegfeld's bride
Anna Held was Florenz Ziegfeld's first star. Demure, with flashing eyes, she married her producer.

Will Rogers in the *Follies*

went crazy trying to figure out why the audience was laughing in the wrong places. When, after about five performances, he discovered the ruse, he solved it in a typical Fields way. He broke the cue over the head of his tormentor, and stretched him out flat. Then he continued the scene as if nothing strange had happened.

Will Rogers had an unusual distinction. He was the only man who could make Ziegfeld laugh. And Florenz admitted it. He knew that he was not supposed to have a very good sense of humor.

Half the great comedians I've had in my shows that I paid a lot of money to and who made my customers shriek were not only not funny to me, but I couldn't understand why they seemed funny to anybody. But this Rogers, I never miss him if I can help it, though you'd be surprised how many of my expensive comics I've run out on and locked myself in my office when they were on stage.

There were others such as Eddie Cantor that Ziegfeld plucked from burlesque, but perhaps the greatest of them all was, I am glad to say, a woman. And the story of Fanny Brice illustrates more perfectly than any other the way that burlesque was a training ground for comedians and the way that Ziegfeld capitalized on that.

It's strange that in a show famous for its long-limbed beauties, the most fa-

Ziegfeld and chorus beauties

mous of them all was a spindly-legged, sad-mouthed, unattractive girl. She triumphed with her mind, her quick wit, her ability to move audiences to both laughter and tears. She was some girl.

She was born Fanny Borach on October 29, 1891 on the shabby Lower East Side, that area from whose concrete soil so many talents blossomed. Her father was a saloon keeper, and her mother made good use of the free lunches of the period. It is said that Fanny, as a child, would stand on the bar and entertain the beer-guzzling troops.

Whether the stories of her bar performances are legend or fact, it is true that Fanny was very early headed for show business. But she had a drawback. She wasn't beautiful, she wasn't even pretty, and this problem became even more apparent when she landed her first big job. It was an eighteen-dollar-a-week job in Seamon's Trans-atlantic burlesque, and the producer, looking at her, decided it would be best if the audience didn't even see her. So he hired her to sing from the balcony, or backstage, or in the wings. Never on stage. But that voice carried her to fame.

Earl Carroll's line-up
In competition with the Ziegfeld girls were these charmers of Earl Carroll's *Vanities*.

The soubrette of the show was about as non-soubrette-looking as one could be. She was fat, and getting along in years, and the audiences started to complain in their usual subtle fashion—by hissing, booing, and throwing things. After the old soubrette, anyone would be an improvement, and the producer finally let Fanny appear on stage. She wowed them. She could mimic anyone, from the Queen of England to Theda Bara. And what she could do with a song!

Irving Berlin, already famous, gave her his song "Sadie Salome" and suggested she sing it in a Yiddish dialect. It was hilariously funny—and yet tearfully sad at the same time. And Ziegfeld, on one of his talent-searching trips, heard her sing that song and hired her on the spot without a second thought.

A great talent had deserted burlesque. That very same year, the little girl considered too ugly to appear on a burlesque stage, starred in a Broadway show with the biggest names in show business. And she became so identified with the *Ziegfeld Follies* that audiences did not think it was an authentic show if she was not in it.

Who today would not give their last show business dollar to see her play just one of her scenes, "Camille," with W. C. Fields? She could leave the audience limp with laughter, and then bring them to tears with a song like "My Man." This was the song which became identified with her; it's a blues song, and Fanny sang it so well because she was authentically blue. She was in love with a handsome gangster named Nicky Arnstein. She stayed in love with him, when he went to jail, and even when he deserted her for other girls after his return. When Fanny would appear in a simple, black dress under a street lamp and sing those wistful words, "Oh my man I love him so, you'll never know," the eyes of the audience, even though glazed from feminine flesh in previous scenes, would fill with tears every time.

Fanny Brice, W. C. Fields, Will Rogers, Eddie Cantor, Leon Errol, and more than a hundred beautiful girls, some of them in nude tableaus. Truly, all of the action was uptown. Downtown, and across the country, burlesque struggled on under the moral restrictions of Sam Scribner, with much of its talent deserting it every day for Broadway. Once again this bawdy, lovable theatre seemed destined for oblivion. But there were stars on the horizon.

The immortal Fanny
Fanny Brice was perhaps the
funniest girl that ever
lived. She is seen in a rare
glamor pose at left. But
her forte was humor, with such
greats as Bobby Clark.

A
pretty
girl
is
like
a
melody

Ann Corio at 16

The origin of the striptease

THE STARS ON THE HORIZON OF BUR-lesque were not blinking—they were stripping. Shedding clothes is women's oldest and most seductive act—but it was a new role as public entertainment. And when those shoulder straps started slipping slowly off snowy flesh, the crowds began to return to the burlesque theatres. Stripteasing, it was called, for the tease was the major element. It gave burlesque new impetus for decades and eventually spread all over the world. So successful has it been that scholars who should be spending their academic hours poring over equations or philosophy have battled instead over the origin of this entertainment—and spent hours looking at the pictures.

Well, who did perform the first strip-tease?

Salome, it has been recorded, danced and removed her clothes so well that King Herod offered her anything she craved. The head of John, the Baptist, on a platter was not too great a prize; after all, John hadn't clapped and whistled when he was supposed to.

Salome was probably not the first, for it was her beauty and ability that were noteworthy, not the act itself. If the records were complete, we might find that that great First Lady, Eve of the fig leaf, started the whole thing. As it is,

we only have a mention of the first reverse strip.

Whether the striptease began with Eve or not, there is no direct line from Eve and Salome to the girls of the twentieth century. There are many stories of how it all began in this country, and I will put down here those origins I have heard and then give you my own idea.

In 1908 Anna Held, the first wife of Florenz Ziegfeld, is reported to have done a disrobing act in a number called "I'd Like to See a Little More of You" at the Mason Opera House in Los Angeles. She took her clothes off behind a screen, which is cheating a bit, but then in 1908 you had to be careful.

In 1913, at the Hippodrome on the Barbary Coast in San Francisco, the "Skevo Brothers" had a girl named simply "Mazie," who undressed *not* behind a screen—but behind a white shadowgraph.

In 1915 at the Academy of Music in Pittsburgh, Mlle. de Leon, the original "Girl in Blue," appeared on stage wearing an old-time opera coat, and carrying a parasol. She then took the coat off and revealed herself in tights and a leotard. This wasn't exactly stripping either, but it was in the right direction. The story I like best about Mlle. de Leon's act occurred the night she couldn't

appear because she was ill. What to do? The manager didn't want to refund that precious box-office money. They pinned the costume on the chorus producer, Bunny Weldon, and he did an impersonation of her, which fooled the audience completely.

Meanwhile, on the motion picture screen in 1916, the "fabulous Vamp," Theda Bara, did an act in the "Dance of the Seven Veils" that had all the elements of a striptease.

Around 1920 a girl named Mae Dix is supposed to have originated a tease number with newspapers, reading headlines and having box-seat patrons tear strips of the paper during each chorus of her number, gradually getting down to a small piece of newspaper to cover her anatomy. Could it have been the sports page?

Around the same time another lass, Margie Bartell, did a tease number with a Spanish shawl in a 1920's Columbia Wheel show titled *Town Scandals*.

There are other stories about a chorus girl's shoulder strap accidently breaking and about a soubrette delaying the entrance of a comic who followed her act by removing pieces of clothing. Whether they are true or not, I just don't know. If they happened at all, they happened far before my time. For my money, the two

71

Theda Bara, "The Vamp"

leading contenders for the title of first stripteaser are Hinda Wassau and Carrie Finnell.

Hinda has a lot of scholars on her side—and why not? She was beautiful, and she was a big star when I first appeared on the scene, clutching my dress, and worried about my mother. Hinda's claim to be the originator stems from a reported occurrence in Chicago at the State-Congress Theatre (some say the Haymarket Theatre) in 1928.

For almost half a century girls on stage had worn tights and leotards. Just around this time, they were daring to come on stage *au naturel*, without tights, just the bare legs showing. At the same time quiver and shimmy numbers were popular. As one historian puts it, "It was inevitable that sooner or later with the constant quiver of the anatomy, somebody was going to lose a part of the costume she was wearing." When she did, there would be only bare flesh showing, and that's just what happened to start the modern striptease—or so the story goes.

Every week at the State-Congress Theatre, the company presented a chorus-girls contest. Hinda Wassau was selected from the chorus to do a shimmy-shaking dance. She wore a short, beaded-fringe costume under the regular chorus costume. When it was her turn, she was to exit to the wings, remove the regular chorus costume, and do her dance with the brief beaded costume. But one night she ran into trouble. When she exited to remove her chorus costume, she couldn't get it off. It was stuck on the costume beneath. Meanwhile the manager was bawling at her to "get on stage," and her music was playing.

Hinda was in a panic. She tore at the costume. No luck. Then, with the manager braying, she went out on stage with the outer costume half on, and half off—and started to do her shimmy dance.

Under the frantic vibrations of her anatomy, the outer costume started to come loose. So she removed as much of it as she could. The audience howled. She shimmied some more—and more of it came loose, and she removed that. By now the audience was with her all the way. At the climax of her number the costume came completely loose and she removed it. The applause at the end of her number was thunderous. But when she was through and went backstage she found a white-lipped manager, who saw his theatre tumbling about him in ruins. "What was that all about?" he cried. "Are you trying to get me closed?"

But that act made Hinda's name and fame. Shortly after, she stepped out of

the chorus and became a featured attraction. She was signed by Texas Guinan, and appeared for seventeen weeks in her New York nightclub. For years she was a star in burlesque.

All of Hinda Wassau's story is so fully documented and the details are so complete that I'm not going to be the one to say it isn't true. It might actually have happened that way. But when I was starting in the business, the one we all looked up to as the mother of the striptease was Carrie Finnell.

Now Carrie wasn't beautiful, the darling; she was—let's face it—fat. But she had pazazz and oomph and the men loved to see her in action. As far as I'm concerned, Carrie invented the striptease because, even if Hinda's story is true, Carrie was the first one to deliberately "tease" the audience. I've always said, anyone can strip, but few can tease. And the tease is the most important part.

Around 1928 Carrie was booked into a theatre in Cleveland, Ohio—and she was looking for a new idea. For one thing, as any stage performer would, she wanted to prolong her booking. It's nicer to eat for eight weeks than for one. Then the great idea came to her. In her first week at the theatre she was billed as an "added attraction." Carrie removed only one

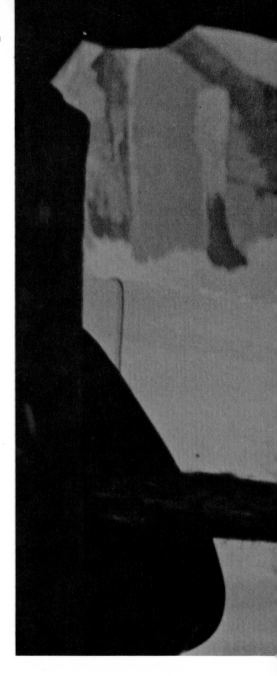

garment and promised the folks there'd be more to come off. Some say that this first garment-shedding incident was an accident; nonetheless, Carrie knew how to take advantage of it. The next week she took off another garment. The third week, she merely shortened another garment. This act, which must still be the record for a striptease anywhere, went on for fifty-two weeks. Carrie had stretched a week's booking into a full year—and originated the "tease."

Carrie was one of the most wonderful women I ever knew. She had a great sense of humor, and she never let anything bother her. She started out as the "Girl with the Million Dollar Legs" and, after she put on weight, she blamed it on inflation. She went on for decades and up to the year she died, not too long ago, she was still charming the boys in the front rows. For one thing, she did something no one has ever done better, and she's had hundreds of imitators. She invented tassel-twirling. No doubt about that. I've never heard anyone even claiming that someone else did it. She became so famous at tassel-twirling that she billed herself as the "Remote Control Girl." And what remote control! She could stand there, still as a statue, and suddenly pop one of her breasts right out of her bodice. As one writer put it, "She has trained each generous bust to

twitch on cue, jump to attention, and do just about everything except sing 'April Showers' in Swahili."

It was Carrie's idea to attach a tassel to the bra cup of each of these educated bosoms, and then let things fly. She would start one tassel on one bosom slowly like a propeller revving up on a World War I plane. Faster and faster it would spin while its fellow tassel lay limp and neglected on the other bosom. Then, the other tassel would come to life. It would start spinning slowly, while the first tassel was at full speed. Carrie looked like a twin-engine bomber. She would walk across stage with the tassels swirling in front of her, and the applause would ring out.

Nowadays, the women in the audience get the biggest kick out of this type of act. I can hear them asking themselves and each other whether they can do it. Carrie could do anything with those tassels. She could make one go slow, the other fast. She could spin the left in one direction, and the right in an opposite direction. She could lie on her back and somehow keep the tassels elevated and twirling. She could attach tassels to her derriere and have them spinning every which way while the bosom tassels revolved merrily on their own. Quite an act had Carrie, and she made it famous for a long, long time.

I can't twirl tassels. I've tried. Nothing happens. My propellers are stalled. If the Germans were closing in, I'd never get off the ground. I salute Carrie as the originator of the striptease, and all burlesque should salute her. Because strip-

teasing came along just in time to save our form of show business when it seemed as if Ziegfeld and his uptown shows were going to drive us out of business.

The tights were gone now. The leo-tards had been removed. Pretty girls had begun to tease and tease the on-lookers by slowly stripping. In no time at all the audiences were coming back to pack the theatres.

When I first started stripping, many of the girls had one of our hard-working tenors in the wings, singing ballads such as "The Sweetheart of Sigma Chi." It was usually a race as to which would split first, the stripper's dress—or her ear drums. Gradually producers did away with the cracked-voice tenors in the wings and substituted music, and most importantly the drummer. I don't know what a stripper would do without that drummer. He controls her movements like a Drill Sergeant—and when the big moments come in her act, he's tattooing that drum like a Civil War drummer at Bull Run.

A word about the costumes. As I've said earlier, they were elaborate. Some were slinky gowns of satin with mink stoles casually tossed around the shoulders. Some were full-hooped dresses of the Southern belle era. Usually, when the girls had shed this outer garment, they would be dressed underneath in a bra and a panel dress. A panel dress consisted of two panels, one in front and one in back secured low around the waist. These the stripper could swirl, or pick up, to show a bit of dazzling leg as she went through her dance. Then, at long last, the bra would come off revealing pasties. A word about pasties. They hurt when you pull them off! How we strippers have suffered over the years—and now how it all seems in vain when you can go in a restaurant and have the girl serving you bend over the table completely nude above the waist. Morality is a funny thing in this country. Where does it draw the line?

For years and years, you could apparently show all of your breast—but lightning would strike if you showed that last tiny half an inch of bosom.

Moving farther south, as the weathermen like to say, we come to another problem. This time I'm on the side of the censors—not just for morality or modesty, although I'm all for the old virtues in their place, and especially the place we're now talking about. I've always said—and, in fact, I was widely quoted on the subject years ago when I was just getting started—that a girl looks sexier in panties than she does nude. I know, because I always ended my act with panties on—and I've never had any objections in the "sexy" department. You burlesque buffs are saying, no doubt, as you read this, "Who's talking about panties? What about the G-string?"

The G-string is as identified with burlesque as the violin with an orchestra. I don't know who invented these gadgets. I don't even know where they got their name. I've seen so many varieties of them that the rhinestones alone could fill the Hudson river and turn it into a road. The G-string—for you lay readers—is a tiny jewel-like bauble on a string around the waist which covers up its specific subject. In truth, many girls

wore flesh-covered gauze, in addition—but then there were some that didn't. Are you listening, Margie Hart? Along with the pasties on the bosom, they were the last garment still attached to the stripper when she finished her act. Hung loosely around the body, the G-string flying up and down added to the excitement when a bump-and-grinder started giving her all. It seemed to be the perfect compromise between what you couldn't show and what you could. Legends grew up around the G-string. One stripper, Rozelle Rowland, is reported to have tied her gold G-string as a wedding ring on the hand of Baron d'Empain. Other strippers painted the G-string with radium paint. When the lights went out, all you could see was the string, and your imagination did the rest.

Some scholars have said that the striptease is the only show-business form ever originated in America. I won't get into arguments about that—there may be others. But I do know we did originate stripteasing—and I do know that it has spread all over the world. The Crazy Horse in Paris is one of the great striptease shows in the world; their acts are creative, beautifully lighted, and much more extravagant than ours. Nevertheless, they imported the idea from Uncle Sam's nieces. At places like the Windmill Theatre in London, they start the striptease shows early in the morning. Why wait for tea? In fact, you can't name many countries in the Western Hemisphere that don't have some theatre or nightclub with strip-tease acts pleasing the customers.

Yes, the United States flag—and those G-strings—are flying all over the world as I write this. I know I sound like a super-patriot but it's nice to know we can export something somewhere—and get some gratitude.

Hinda Wassau, Carrie Finnell—and suddenly stripteasing was the rage, and every chorus girl, including me, wanted to be a star. Well, it wasn't as easy as all that. And out of thousands of in-genues with an urge to strip, only a few girls became famous throughout the land. But famous they did become. For almost two decades their names would be as familiar to the American public as movie stars. Gypsy Rose Lee, Margie Hart, Georgia Sothern, Lois DeFee— even today, for nostalgic men over thirty, these are names to conjure with. They—and others—became the great girls of burlesque. I was destined to be one, too. But if anyone had told me that while I was teaching Sunday School in Hartford, I would have died on the spot.

I came,
I saw,
I fainted

ALL MY LIFE I'VE LOOKED AT PEOPLE WHO had an unspoken question in their eyes. What they seemed to want to ask is, "How can a nice girl, brought up in a good Catholic family, take her clothes off in public?" Believe me, it wasn't easy. Little did I know when I got into show business how much I would have to "show!"

It all began when I was a six-year-old in Hartford, Connecticut, and saw my first stage show, a traveling vaudeville company. A kindly neighbor took me. She had box seats, and since I'd never been to a theatre before I thought we were to sit on boxes. When I saw that stage lit up, and heard the people applaud, I was hooked. From that moment on, I knew I wanted to be in show business. What I didn't know is amusing in retrospect. I had a problem that Helen Hayes, for example, didn't have. Both of us wanted to perform, but Helen had what I consider an unfair advantage. She could act.

This is as good a time as any to salute — and apologize to — a grand group of people. I am thinking of the thousands of wonderful patrons of the theatre who paid their way into summer theatre shows to see me perform in such legitimate dramas as *Cat on a Hot Tin Roof.* I guess I didn't look too bad running around in a slip, but when it came to those tense scenes and crackling dialogue, I left something to be desired. One thing is positive. They came to *see* my lines, not *hear* them!

Actually, I never had many complaints, as I look back. In fact, in at least one legitimate play, my dialogue tore the house down with applause. That was when I would appear in *White Cargo* in a college town such as Cambridge, Mass. My entire speaking part in the first act consisted of one line. Just as the first act ended, I would undulate on stage dressed only in a very brief loin-cloth, and some brown powder, pose wickedly in front of the white hunter, and murmur, "I am Tondelayo!"

At this, a Harvard boy jumped to his feet and shouted, "My God, what an actress!"

Incidentally, in those legitimate shows I was much more undressed than I had ever been in burlesque. In my strip-tease numbers, I had had a pale, lavendar light to shield me and a very sheer leotard with a few rhinestones splashed in strategic places. In *White Cargo*, when I made my entrance, I was nude from the waist up, all lights blazing on stage; but I did wear about eight ounces of brown powder and the loincloth. Later, in another legitimate show, I was asked to do a bump and grind. I told the astonished producer that I had never done a bump and grind in burlesque. He was clever. He told me that Katharine Cornell would do a bump and grind if the part called for it. I agreed to it. Burlesque, as well as the legitimate stage, however, were far in the future for that six-year-old in Hartford, Connecticut.

I came from a happy family, but a large one. At the dinner table, you could get your arm broken reaching for a slice of bread. I guess that's why my Italian mother, busy trying to raise her children, didn't see the signs in time. She couldn't watch all of us every minute — and after school when she thought I was playing with the other children, I'd be hiking downtown to hang around the theatre. I got to be a pet of the performers, and they'd often let me stand in the wings and savor the color and applause. Once I was even allowed into a dressing room to watch an actress apply her makeup. I acted in school and church plays as I grew up, dreaming about show business, but never thinking I would one day actually be a part of it. I was a freshman in high school in a town dominated by insurance companies. On Sundays I was teaching the prayer class at St. Lawrence O'Toole's church. My future was all planned in the actuarial tables:

marriage, children, death—all in Hartford.

Then my life burst out of its dreams when a letter arrived. It was from a girl friend who had gone to New York in the summer. She was in the chorus of a Broadway show. Broadway! And they were looking for more girls! Me! My mother took this news with the same enthusiasm Napoleon felt about the first snowflake outside of Moscow. The storm was underway all right—and my retreat from Hartford. In those days, to an Italian mother, show business was a place for fallen women. Had I said I was resigning from the faith, she couldn't have been more shocked. But New York, the great big magnet to the south, was pulling against my mother's iron will—and the magnet won out. She finally agreed to let me go.

It was a Shubert touring show, and I was hired on the spot. Thirty-five dollars a week. What was more important, I was in show business.

I was also in Hell—the private Hell of a fifteen-year-old away from home for the first time. I was, to say the least, homesick. I called my mother after only two weeks and said I wanted to return home. I was afraid to tell the manager, so Mama sent me the fare, which she could ill afford (we were playing in Har-

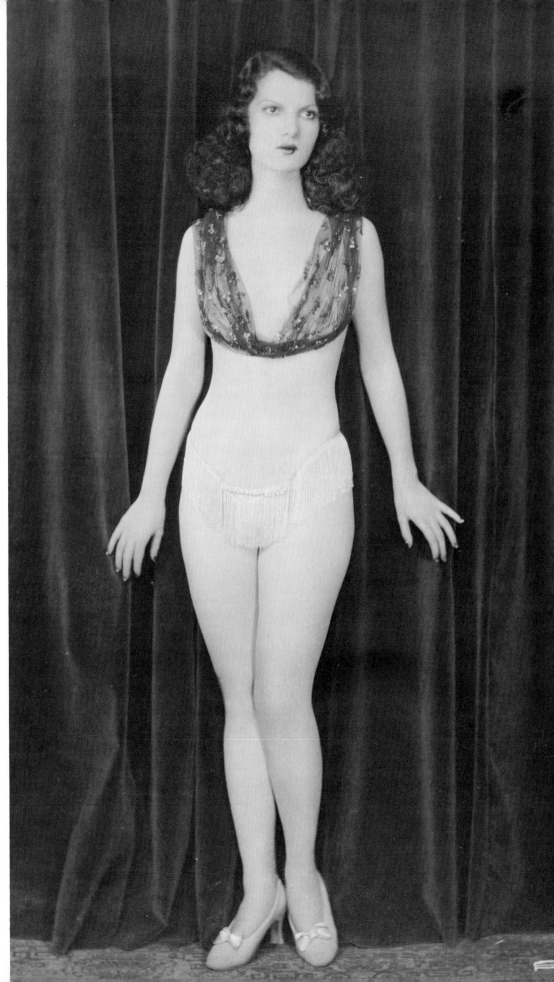

Burlesque newcomer
Ann Corio looks a bit wide-eyed after first joining a burlesque chorus.

risburg, Pennsylvania). But Annina (as Mama called me) was coming back to the fold—and she had that nice Italian boy picked out for me already.

Life, however, takes strange turns. What if I had not quit that first show? I probably would have stayed in Broadway choruses, studied acting, and made a quite different life for myself, all outside of burlesque. And I'd have missed a lot of fun.

As it was, I went back to Hartford and some weeks later heard from my girl friend again. This time she wrote that she was in a chorus at a burlesque show. You will have to take my word on faith— I truly didn't know what burlesque was. I had never seen it because burlesque shows never played Hartford. I thought it was another form of vaudeville. Luckily for me, my mother didn't know either, and soon I was on my way to New York and burlesque.

Stripteasing was already in full swing when I arrived, and my eyes opened wide. What kind of show business was this? Girls were taking off their clothes and making gestures never seen in church plays. Comics were saying jokes that men usually told only in private stag parties.

But a funny thing happened. I found myself laughing at the jokes. How could

I not? Those comics in tramp uniforms and putty noses were hilarious, although the first one I saw, Billy "Scratch" Wallace, actually frightened me when I saw that putty nose. Then I noticed something else. I was wearing less clothes in the chorus than the featured stripper at the end of her act. In actual fact, I was showing more and enjoying less money. While I was still trying to put these two facts together, the company manager bawled out one day to the chorus girls: "Anybody speak French?" He was looking for a girl to play in a scene. I immediately shouted, *"Oui."* It was the right answer and a lucky one for me because it was the only French I knew. Naturally, it turned out it was all I needed, because in burlesque scenes the girls never say, *"Non."*

Now I found myself slightly above the chorus-girl level, after only a few days. The company manager liked me—I was a fresh, pretty girl of fifteen—and made me the soubrette, which is the leading chorus girl. I was featured in every number. I must have done all right, because the manager asked me if I wanted to do a striptease number in the next show. The pay was almost double. I wrestled with my conscience and my pocketbook and you know who always wins *that* match.

But what would I do? I didn't like those bumps and grinds. I conceived an act based around the one virtue that drives men wild: innocence! I would be a pretty little girl with ruffled skirt, carrying a pail of candy kisses. I'd skip down the runway singing, "Give me a little kiss," as I threw out the candy.

All very pretty, but one thing was wrong. I had no costume, and no money to buy one. So I went to work. I sewed a little bra and a skirt of ruffles. All week long I didn't sleep because I was sewing on those damn ruffles. But I did it.

Opening day, the show was running too long, so my number was cut. Just like that! Now *I* was ruffled. I quit. Billy Koud, the choreographer at the Irving Place Theatre at the time, asked me to come back and I would be a principal.

I was a hit right away? And why not? I was a fifteen-year-old girl competing against strippers who were mostly in their late thirties or forties. People liked my act. That innocent approach always gets through to the boys with evil in their hearts. The more innocent I was, the more wicked they felt, and the more often they paid their way through the turnstiles. My salary started going up and up. Soon I was making more money than I had ever known existed. Then, Broadway came to pay me a call.

Neophyte to star
Ann left the chorus line
almost immediately to become a
striptease star. At right
she is seen at the peak
of her career.

Ann Corio, the First Lady

I wanted to be a legitimate actress. Earl Carroll's *Vanities* at that time was a big hit in New York. And I got a call to visit the big producer's office. There was another man there; I've forgotten his name. Two things soon became apparent to me. If I joined the Earl Carroll show, there might be some extracurricular duties involved with friends of the producer. And, second, the salary was about half of what I was making in burlesque. And yet, an appearance on Broadway might lead to bigger things.

I went through one of those agonizing periods people have when faced with a crucial decision. It was obvious that I was going to make big, big money in burlesque; I was already deluged with offers from producers to head my own show. But I wanted to be a legitimate actress. In the end, I decided I'd be better off in burlesque. I doubt that the stage lost a potential Sarah Bernhardt, but one thing I know for sure: I made the right decision. Although I didn't dream it then, in time I was to become famous— and have a lot of fun while doing it. That's a pretty nice blueprint for a career.

This fame and fun was all ahead of me when I decided to return to burlesque, but I had to have a few shattering experiences first. Remember, I was fresh from Hartford—and no one

1936—91st Season of the Old Howard—1937

HOWARD ATHENAEUM

TEL. CAPITOL 1565
Always something doing from 9.00 A. M. until 11 P. M.
3 Complete Burlesque Shows Daily: 12 Noon; 2.30 P. M. and 8.30 P. M.
MIDNIGHT SHOW EVERY FRIDAY, 11.30 P. M.

Week of January 25, 1937
EXTRA-ADDED ATTRACTION
HER MAJESTY -- The QUEEN
ANN CORIO

And The
"GIRLS from TOYLAND" Burlesquers---with

BILLY ARLINGTON	DOT A'HEARN	PEANUTS BOHN
JEAN ROSE	BOB BATES	JOAN MARVIS	KENZA VINTON
JACK RYAN	THREE LaMAR BROS.
RICHARD and MARTIN TWINS IN "DANCEOLOGY"

COMING — WEEK OF FEBRUARY 8th
Sensational Muff Dancer -- YVETTE

PARADE OF STARS COMING SOON TO THE OLD HOWARD

JOE DeRITA	MANNY KING	MAE BROWN
BILLY HAGAN	JOHNNY BARRY	DOROTHY WAHL
HARRY CONNOLLY	BOZO SNYDER	SUNYA SLANE
BILLY "Beef Trust" WATSON	FRANK SILK	GEORGIA SOUTHERN
HONEY BEE KELLAR	VERNE	EVELYN WHITNEY
	JERRY MACAULEY	

NOTHING TOO GOOD FOR OLD HOWARD PATRONS

The Queen is announced…

in my family knew what I was doing. They thought I was an actress in some kind of play.

One afternoon I was on stage doing my act. I was halfway undressed when I saw a face in the second row that made me stop cold. There sat my mother. She had slipped into town without telling me, just to check up.

To give you an idea of my mother's strictness, she never even allowed me to smoke a cigarette. It was too sinful. She used to say, "Italian girls don't smoke!" This gave me a laugh years later when I took my mother on a sentimental trip to Italy, her first re-visit to her country. I noticed all around us that the girls in Rome were smoking. I needled her. I said, "Mama, you always told me Italian girls don't smoke."

Quick as a flash, she answered, "They're not Italian!"

So, here I was, her innocent girl who should be protected from all vices, taking off her clothes in public! The storm broke backstage after the performance. She really let me have it. Her dream was that I would return to Hartford and marry a nice, hard-working Italian boy.

My dreams lay elsewhere. But I sought to comfort her. I told her that in burlesque, unlike nightclubs, the girls were on stage, far removed from men. I told

The Queen arrives

her that I never revealed more than you could see on any public beach. All of this was true. My mother saw it was hopeless to dissuade a star-struck daughter. Finally, she took all my arguments into consideration and said I could go on undressing under one condition.

"Just so they look-a, but no touch!"

I guess that's been my motto ever since.

The great girls

DURING ALL THE YEARS OF THE HEYDAY of burlesque, I was billed as the "Queen." I got reams of publicity, I made amounts of money based on percentage of the gross that were staggering, people asked for my autograph, and limousines with hopeful millionaires parked near my dressing room door. But I'd be the first to admit that I never made it as big as Gypsy Rose Lee.

Gypsy had a fair body—nothing sensational—but she had sensational brains and a beautiful face. She knew what she was doing at all times. She exploited the tease factor of striptease to the limit. She wore colorful costumes, red garters, black silk stockings. She looked feminine, and she made every small disrobing act a challenge to the viewer. Those stockings seemed to take forever coming off.

It really wasn't her disrobing technique that was so appealing—it was her attitude. She seemed to be saying to the men, "I know what you want, boys— we're adults, aren't we?" She'd talk to them from the stage, say witty things, and always seemed to be in control.

The fact is, she never took much off— but she seemed to be shedding plenty, because of the suggestiveness of her act, her expression, and her remarks. The act was full of charm. In later years she liked to say she was really spoofing the whole thing. Maybe she was, but the men didn't know that at the time. All they saw was a beautiful, intelligent girl who smiled wryly as she undressed before the common man.

That's my analysis anyway, although I've heard arguments for years about the secret of Gypsy's success. Many of the other strippers were jealous of her; *they* took their clothes off in all good faith, bumped and ground and writhed till they were exhausted—and no one asked *them* to rub shoulders with Alexander Woollcott.

The intellectuals delighted in Gypsy. I guess they saw in her the perfect compromise between sex and brains (every intellectual I've met thinks he, himself, is that perfect compromise). She became the favorite of the avant-garde and the cafe-society crowd. As a result, Gypsy wasn't in burlesque too long, although she was forever identified with it. As a further evidence of her intelligence, Gypsy made a lot of money out of that identification.

She went on to Ziegfeld shows, and nightclub revues, and then the legitimate theatre in such productions as Mike Todd's *Peep Show* and *Star and Garter,* which were really glorified burlesque. She wrote a best-selling book called *The G-String Murders.* Then she wrote her memoirs, *Gypsy,* which was made into a sensational musical and movie. If I wore a hat, I'd take it off to Gypsy, for I admire her. In a way, she did us all a favor because she proved that stripteasers could have brains along with their more well-known attributes.

Margie Hart, another of the great striptease stars, went clear to the other side of the horizon. She was strictly something for the boys, and they knew it and

Brainy and beautiful
Gypsy Rose Lee always had brains to go with her beauty. After leaving burlesque, she became the pet of an intellectual crowd.

Gypsy Rose Lee, zip!

The Gypsy touch
Gypsy Rose Lee emphasized
the "tease," making witty
chatter to the audience
while her garments seemed to
take forever coming off.

loved her for it. Margie was a dazzling redhead, with a beautiful body, and she didn't mind showing it. Years later that got all of burlesque in trouble, but in the intervening years it paid off big.

Margie didn't wear a G-string, most of the time. You'd be surprised how this adds to the suspense if the boys up front know this fact. Margie would wear one of those panel dresses mentioned earlier; the panels covered everything up all right, but Margie would take her little hands and swish that dress around a bit—just enough to pull the boys to the edge of their seats. She caused more eye-strain in one night than the New York Eye Hospital sees in a year.

Margie was billed as "The Poor Man's Garbo," but she didn't "vant to be alone." She wanted a theatre filled with men—and she got it. She was the most daring stripper of them all, and there were always men on hand hoping that *this* night she would be more daring than she ever was before.

She did a traditional strip, with only that suggestion of nudity beneath, which no other stripper I knew dared. With those panels swirling she gave the boys what they came to see: flashes so brief that they didn't really reveal anything, but that suggested all.

It pleases me to say that Margie, our most daring stripper at the time, may now well be our most "proper" alumna. When Mayor La Guardia banned burlesque in New York, she stayed on the circuit only a few years, then abruptly left it all behind and retired to a life as a suburban housewife in Bel Air, California. When she left, she left—not like a girl named Ann Corio, who just can't seem to leave burlesque behind. Margie never came out of retirement no matter what the temptation. A few years ago when I needed a replacement for myself in *This Was Burlesque* during a spell of illness, I telephoned Margie and asked her to come back just this once. She said she was happy in retirement, and I'm glad for her.

Another great redheaded star of those days—and today one of my best friends—was Georgia Sothern. Georgia stripped and Georgia teased, but that was only a minor part of her act. Her music, "Hold That Tiger," was wild, the orchestra played at full-blast and full tempo, and Georgia came on stage in full flight. And she'd work up momentum. Faster and faster the music would roar, and Georgia would be at the front of the stage, one hand cascading her long red hair over her face, the other outstretched to keep her balance as her hips blurred back and forth at a fantastic tempo. It was exhila-

rating, exciting — even forgetting the sex appeal involved. The mere sight of this red-hot, redheaded temptress tossing her hips in fantastic abandon to the wild music of the band caught up everybody in a spell. You didn't shout from the audience to Georgia to take it off; there was no time, no cause, and the music was too loud, anyway. You just sat there and watched — and wondered how she could do it.

By the time she was finished, the whole theatre seemed to explode in a sigh. The audience was almost as exhausted watching as Georgia was performing. She did an act that no one who ever saw would ever forget; she was a cyclone of sex and she literally blew the walls down.

Not the biggest name in burlesque during those years, but certainly the tallest was Lois DeFee. Lois was six feet four inches tall, which is a lot of inches — and she had a figure which was perfect for the height. She also had a talent for publicity. Legend has it that Lois started as a bouncer at The Dizzy Club on New York's then-swinging 52nd Street. Somebody at the famous cabaret Leon and Eddie's across the street must have noticed her, because she was soon hired for an unusual job in that cafe.

A daring favorite
Margie Hart was the darling of New York audiences. She was pretty—and more than a little bit naughty.

As Lois described it to a reporter years later:

At that age my contemporaries were just starting to develop mammary glands, but I'd been wearing full-cup brassieres for two years. Anyway it — or they — helped to give the owners of Leon and Eddie's the idea for a sweater-girl gimmick. My job was to walk through the club wearing tight slacks and sweater, with LEON sewed over one breast and EDDIE over the other. I used to wonder what would've happened if the bosses had taken in another partner!

From there, in 1939, she went off to the New York World's Fair where she became the Queen of the Glamazons in the Amazon exhibit. Walter Winchell spotted her there — at six-feet-four she would have been hard to miss — and she soon was on her way to stardom as a burlesque stripteaser. Lois' act made the most out of her tall, statuesque height. As every theatrical producer knows, on the stage tall girls look best, and Lois DeFee certainly qualified in that department. She did what I can only describe as a regal strip — from her queenly heights the garments flowed gently down, while the peasants outside applauded. She was quiet and unhurried; what was there to hurry about? She never did any torso-bumping.

But when she was down to pasties and G-string she was a whole Eiffel Tower of girl standing there before the men. In fact, Winchell billed her as "The Eiffel Eyeful."

The mentions of Winchell in this story remind me of Lois' talent for publicity. She would do nearly anything to make the newspapers. Harry Richman, one of the great names in show business history, had once told her, "When a girl wants to make it in show business, and she's not sure of her talent, then publicity will help."

Did I say Lois liked publicity? When things were at a lull for her on one occasion, she decided to get married — and the wedding was front-page news in every newspaper in the land. For Lois, the Eiffel Eyeful, married a *midget*. The marriage only lasted a few days, but how long does it take to make a photograph? Funnily enough, many, many years after that so-called marriage happened, the jokes it inspired are still with us.

"How did that midget make love to Lois DeFee?"

"Someone put him up to it."

Hinda Wassau, whom I described earlier as the possible originator of the modern striptease, remained a top star throughout the thirties. Hinda's act was sinuous; she paid attention to her body and made certain the men paid attention, too. In case they forgot, she would

Tall story
Lois DeFee (*left*) a striptease star who towered more than six feet, was once billed as "The Eiffel Eyeful."

Tiger girl
The dynamic Georgia Sothern did her number to the music of "Hold That Tiger." And when her hips blurred into motion, the crowd would roar its approval.

use her hands to smooth down her tummy, flirt with her magnificent bosom, all the time panting and making little giggling sounds that might sound funny on an LP record, but sure were sexy when a beautiful girl is proceeding to undress.

Hinda was the first stripper to expose the bosom. She wore a negligee—sheer top—the waist to the floor made of chiffon petals. She'd tease with that negligee—put it on backwards so the outline of her bosom was even more clearly seen through the material. This was even sexier than exposing herself completely, as any striptease star can tell you. And at the finish of her act she'd give the boys a quick flash—that ultimate revelation of the bosom in an instant which leaves the audience wondering if it was a dream.

Faith Bacon was another well-known name of the time. She claimed to have originated the fan dance, and maybe she did, although the fan dance is as closely identified with Sally Rand as the G-string to burlesque. Sally, you might be surprised to hear, never played burlesque—until we hired her to fill in for me at one time in *This Was Burlesque*. I never saw Faith do her act, but I know from eyewitnesses it was the same as Sally's. It is a beautiful act to watch.

95

Faith Bacon, a total beauty

The fan dance is not a striptease; it's a dance as graceful as a ballet. The dancer appears with two huge ostrich-feather fans, one in each hand. These fans are adroitly placed at all times; they cover and they reveal at the whim of the dancer. There's always flesh exposed in this dance, but fleetingly—and with the fans swooping hither and yon, the audience must feel like a peeping tom in the middle of an ostrich farm.

It was always thrilling to me to see Sally Rand work; she had grace in her movements, and true beauty in her dance. When, at the climax of her act, she would throw up her fans like the statue of Winged Victory, she brought the house down with applause.

I understand Sally also did a version of this act with a big balloon instead of ostrich fans in nightclubs. How she managed to avoid those naughty men with lighted cigarettes and pins, I don't know. I wouldn't have the nerve to try it myself. I know men too well.

The names I have mentioned were the big stars in burlesque through that period. They made the most money and received the most acclaim. But there were many other great girls, some of them beautiful, some of them talented, many of them with gimmicks. For one reason or another, maybe just bad luck,

Sally's fans
Sally Rand did not originate the fan dance, but she made it famous. She was the sensation of the Chicago World's Fair in the thirties— and is still doing her fan dance today.

Lily's lock
Lily St. Cyr, here
decked out provocatively
in lock and chain,
is one of the modern
striptease stars
who came along in the
fifties, some years
after the real
heyday of burlesque.

they never reached the heights that the top stars reached, but I'd like, for the record, to salute them now.

Rosita Royce had a charming act, "The Dance of the Doves." She had trained doves which would fly on stage and alight on her arms and shoulders and head while she danced. It made a pretty picture.

Tirza had a different gimmick. She took a "wine bath" on stage. A fountain of wine from a mechanical device would spray and flood down her in such a manner that nothing really important was revealed. For the occasional wino who wandered into our audiences, Tirza's act was heaven.

Incidentally, there was a reported feud between Rosita Royce and Tirza, when they were appearing at the New York World's Fair. One day Tirza turned on her shower of wine—and no wine came out, leaving her dry, bare—and angry. She suspected strongly that a friend of her rival, Rosita Royce, had put gum in the shower holes. Not to be outdone, it is said, pals of Tirza were present when Rosita did her next number with the doves, and peppered the doves with BB shot, causing them to fly off into the blue, leaving Rosita dry, bare—and angry.

A stripper named Yvette Dare went

Reginald Marsh's "Strip Tease"

one better in the bird department. She used a trained parrot in her dance. The parrot would fly about her, plucking off her clothing. Whatever that parrot was after, it was not a cracker.

Zorita is remembered today for her snake act. This idea, as old as Adam and Eve, of a serpent in contact with a beautiful girl was an eye-stopper. Everyone knew the snake was not poisonous, neither was it a boa constrictor; still there was something sensational in the appearance of one snake—and sometimes many more—twined around the arms and legs of a pretty girl performing a daring dance.

Zorita once made a film of her snake act, and revealed that her attitude toward those snakes was actually religious. "I am doing this motion picture," she said, "because it contains such a powerful sermon, telling us all to be on guard against the beast within us, as well as the reptiles without. I consider it my moral duty."

We could have used Zorita in our Cleopotroast and Julius Sneezer scene, especially when Julius comes on stage to find Cleo sobbing. "What's wrong," he asks.

"I lost my asp!"

"*You lost your asp!* But I can see it right there!"

Zorita could have made Cleo's death scene a real production, without losing her asp.

Rose La Rose was a demure and charming girl offstage, but a bit naughty on stage. She recited lyrics telling about her dates with various movie stars while she removed her clothing. She had a tendency to remove too much, but her act was pretty and the boys never objected. It's reported that her husband must have liked her act, too, because when he and Rose were divorced the newspapers said that the doting husband insisted every night that Rose do a strip to a harmonica solo for six choruses. Whether this is true or not, it's a nice plug for Rose—and harmonicas.

Sally Keith, next to Carrie Finnell, was the best tassel-twirler I ever saw. She didn't have Carrie's huge bosoms and fantastic muscular control, but she could make those tassels spin with a fury. For years after she left burlesque she owned and appeared in a nightclub in Scollay Square in Boston, not far from my favorite theatre, the Old Howard. I used to see her from time to time there, and the audience was always filled with students of the art.

Peaches Strange was the "Queen of the Quiver." She had wonderful stomach and hip control; when she quivered, a subtle vibration built up in her body and the audience alike. Since the days of Little Egypt men have been fascinated with the quiver; and I'm fascinated, too—because one of my chorus numbers in our show features a chorus girl who must quiver. Believe me, it isn't as easy as you think, because I've sometimes gone through the whole chorus line, all of them trained dancers, and not found one who could do it. If you don't believe me, ask your wife to quiver tonight.

For all of the many, many girls, the successful and the less-successful, those mentioned here and those I have omitted, I want to make a recommendation which may come as a surprise.

The stripteasers of the thirties were the reigning sex symbols of their time, but their acts, though sexy, were basically innocent. They disrobed. They teased the men to the point of desperation. They even "flashed" a bit more flesh than they should from time to time. But how innocent they were can only be described in terms of their latter-day namesakes, the strippers of today, who work mostly in nightclubs and call themselves "exotics."

When I was preparing to bring burlesque back to Broadway, I visited some of these clubs, and I was appalled. I couldn't believe what had happened. No

A bit of Sherry
Regally beautiful Sherry Britton is a comparatively late arrival in burlesque

The tassel-twirler
Sally Keith, a
jaunty blonde performer,
is best remembered
for her tassel twirling.

A rose is La Rose
Rose La Rose hides
behind some masks—and
no one is fooled.
One or more of these
masks must have been
missing when her
performance was raided
by Boston police.

103

Hot Pepper
A modern stripper
of superb form
is Pepper Powell.

Parrot actors
Yvette Dare had
an act in which
trained parrots
plucked her clothing
off bit by bit.

The love doves
Rosita Royce appeared
with white doves
that fluttered about
her, giving audiences
only brief glimpses
of Rosita's flesh.

The Dean of strippers
Myrna Dean, one of the
prettiest of strippers,
reclines gracefully
for a glamor photograph.

longer was the striptease the mere re-
moval of garments in a sexy way. Now
all of the girls were working with props,
most of which were so obscene I won't
even describe them.

I guess it was desperation. In the lean
years, between the time when Mayor
La Guardia banned burlesque in New
York and today, the girls—probably
under the urging of those money-hungry
nightclub managers—had to work harder
and harder to draw the crowds in. Besides, movies, magazines, Broadway
shows and topless revues might have
made stripteasing seem too tame, and
passé.

Well, I have news for those who feel
this way. The power of sex is the power
of suggestion. Take a glove off in the
right manner, and a man will ask you to
marry him. A woman's greatest asset is
a man's imagination.

The great girls of my time, Gypsy,
Georgia, Margie and all the others, didn't
need any obscene props to get their mes-
sages across. They came out from the
wings and transfixed that audience in a
hypnotic state of adoration, anticipation,
and golden dreams.

I see them now as I saw them then, my
compatriots: Georgia, with her red hair
flying and her hips blurring; Gypsy, with
a subtle smile, tugging at a red garter;

Parks—and recreation
Valerie Parks wears
black stockings,
minute negligee, and
a come-hither look.

Margie, swirling her skirt so that a bright flash of flesh would dazzle the audience; and Carrie, the twin-engine bomber, bringing the boys alive with her tassels. Yes, they were great girls.

Those adorable comics

THE GREAT GIRLS BROUGHT BURLESQUE back from oblivion, but they did something more for America, too: they gave people a chance to enjoy some of the funniest comics who have ever been on any stage.

Earlier in this book I wrote about the great comics such as W.C. Fields who went on to bigger success in other entertainment media. But there were some comedians who never left burlesque who had—in some ways—just as much talent. I know for a fact that they got just as many laughs, because I worked with them and heard the audiences break up. It was these men who made burlesque comedy an enduring tradition in this country. No history of

Dial FUN
Comics in outlandish costumes cavort with pretty chorus girls in the Broadway show, *Top Banana*.

burlesque would be complete without a salute to their talents.

Before my time there were comics such as Bozo Snyder, one of the greatest pantomimists ever; and Sliding Billy Watson, who would come tearing across stage in a slide before beginning a scene. There were also dialect comics such as Benny "Wop" Moore, who could speak broken Italian better than my mother—and who was Jewish.

In my day, the greatest comic of them all was Mike Sachs. His is a wonderful story, not only of humor, but of courage. Mike was the darling of Boston; it was his home base. He played all over, but he always came back to the Old Howard.

Not only was he hilariously funny, but he was also very talented musically. He played a mean piano. He was the most versatile of the great comics.

He was a short and stocky fellow, and he played all of his scenes opposite a tall, elegant straight-woman, Alice Kennedy. Throughout much of his career, his distinguishing feature was cross-eyes. He had one good eye, and one bad.

Alice was a brunette who could affect an elegance that would contrast hilariously with baggy-pants Mike. They'd perform a funny music scene, with her as the singer. She'd hit a couple of ear-piercing high notes and say: "That's my high register. I also have a low register—or maybe you would prefer my *middle register*."

Mike would say, "Oh, hell, yes!" Then the good eye would go back and forth, and the audience would scream.

Mike never resorted to any gestures—nothing physical. His verbal expressions were all double-entendre, but he never did what I call "drawing pictures" to hit someone over the head. He was never vulgar. My theory is, respect the audience's intelligence. If you embarrass them by belaboring a joke, you will lose them and be unable to get them back for five or ten minutes.

Mike never lost the audience. They were with him all the way, especially when he would look at them with that expression that seemed to say, "What hit me?"

Well, something did hit Mike, a horrible tragedy. Right in the middle of his career, he went blind. There must be other performers in the history of entertainment who continued to act on stage after going blind. I don't know any, but I do know Mike. In fact, I worked with him after his blindness. The truth is, Mike worked for years and years, doing every comedy scene he had ever performed before, while totally blind, and still moving that one eye back and forth to point up a gag.

How did he do it? For one thing he knew those scenes so well he could do them in his sleep. For another, he knew the stages of the theatres, every crack and loose board, from years of working. And for still another, he had a loyal talking woman, Alice Kennedy, who stayed with him throughout.

The happy payoff is that Mike did these scenes so well that many people in the audience never realized he was blind. One of those was Irving Berlin who couldn't believe that the fellow on stage, moving so briskly through a scene, was without sight. It was quite a moving moment for Mike when Irving Berlin came backstage afterwards to compliment him on his unconquerable courage. For that's what it was.

Almost every city had its King of Comedy, its particular favorite. As Boston had its Mike Sachs, Philadelphia had—and still has—the immortal Billy "Cheese 'n' Crackers" Hagan. Billy got his "Cheese 'n' Crackers" slogan from his father, a man who never used profanity. If his father hit his thumb with a hammer, he'd say, "Cheese 'n' Crackers." Years later when Billy was on stage and an ad-lib situation came up, he blurted out the phrase, and it became forever identified with him. Billy's

makeup was in the great tradition of burlesque comics. He wore a big putty nose. This, together with his baggy pants, was his costume. What made him even funnier was his high-pitched voice. To hear him, when a beautiful blonde did a wild bump and grind, say "Cheese 'n' Crackers" was just absolutely priceless.

One of the little-known greats of burlesque was Steve Mills. I played with him many times around the Wheel and knew his talent. So when I opened our revival, I sent for him to be our Top Banana. Steve was another versatile comic. In our show, for example, he played a baggy-pants comic in the opening scene; later on he did a comedy strip which was hilarious; then dressed rather smartly—but still with sagging trousers—he sang a duet with the straight man that sometimes brought tears to a nostalgic audience. In the Second Act, he played a white hunter in one scene and the night watchman later in the Crazy House. Steve was the master of the double-take. He'd take out a cigarette just before a funny line, place it in his mouth, and when the straight man said the funny line he'd take the cigarette out of his mouth and hold it transfixed in the air, as if paralyzed. When we played at the Huntington-Hartford Theater in Los Angeles, Cecil Smith, the reviewer, described Steve as follows:

Mills has a face like a lump of dough left behind by some forgetful baker with a couple of evil little eyes in the creases and a slash of mouth through which a single tooth flashes in lonely splendor. His pants are eight sizes too big and they rise only to his knees and his flowery necktie drags the floor.

His timing is incredible. If his art is the art of the wicked leer, the smirk, the gesture that makes a seemingly innocent statement lewd and gamy, nonetheless he is an absolute master at it. Even when the jokes seem old, his artistry makes them fresh.

That's my Steve.

It is very difficult to say who was the funniest of all the great comics, but certainly none was funnier than Charlie Robinson. Charlie was a very small man who probably weighed about eighty pounds, including his car keys. One critic called him "Jiminy Cricket"—and, indeed, with his large, hollow eyes and black bangs over his forehead he seemed about to hop somewhere.

Charlie was a master of pantomime. His big sketch was "The Gun Ain't Loaded." This is one of the most hilarious scenes ever done—and it is so basic. Charlie is a traveling salesman whose car breaks down in front of a farmhouse. Two love-starved girls are the only occupants of the house. But they show him a big shotgun and tell him it's loaded,

Bozo the Tramp
Bozo Snyder was perhaps the best pantomime artist ever to appear on the old burlesque stage.

111

"So don't try anything."

As soon as Charlie goes to sleep, however, one scantily-clad young thing pops into the room and beckons him to follow her. He does, gladly, and while he's offstage the second girl pops into the room from the other side of the stage and wonders where that cute little fellow is. Back he comes, and the other girl must have him. Back he comes after this second experience, and he is a changed man. His knees buckle, he leans and pulls against the drapes to keep erect, he barely makes it back to bed—and there's the first girl, ready for another go. Poor Charlie. By now the audience is with him all the way. Gamely, reluctantly, but inevitably, he forces himself to his wobbly feet and staggers off after the girl. This time, when he returns, he is in a wheelbarrow—a crumpled ruin of a man whom the girl contemptuously dumps onto the bed on his face. You should hear the audience roar with laughter. Charlie, being so small and pathetic-looking, only made it seem more real.

Rags Ragland was another talented baggy-pants comic. His only problem was that—despite the baggy pants—he was enormously attractive to women.

This led to a funny surprise for Abbott and Costello one night. They were doing the Crazy House scene at the Shubert Theatre in Philadelphia. There is absolutely no funnier scene in show business than the Crazy House. It's been absorbed in dozens of ways on different shows. One of the most popular shows of recent years on television, Rowan and Martin's "Laugh-In," is nothing more than an expanded Crazy House scene.

The Crazy House is a series of blackouts that take place in front of one befuddled man: the newly hired guard at an insane asylum. The nurse tells him to guard the door and not let any crazy characters escape. He nervously goes to bed—and through the door comes character after character, all crazy.

Sample: A Chinaman staggers in.
CHINAMAN:
Me Confucius! I tell you great saying.
COMIC:
What is your great saying?
CHINAMAN *(Pompously)*:
He who flingee dingee, flingee dingee!
COMIC *(Double-take)*:
Ah, but don't forget. He who flingee dingee must have dingee to flingee!

In another blackout a drunk staggers on stage holding a whiskey bottle in his hand. The comic sees the man is hopelessly drunk, and deftly steals the bottle, raises it to his lips, and starts gulping the liquid. The drunk turns, sees him, and shouts, "Don't drink that! I'm taking it to the doctor!"

Mills, starting out

Top Banana
Steve Mills, the Top Banana
in *This Was Burlesque* when
it opened in New York, captivated
legitimate reviewers, some of
whom had never seen an authentic
baggy-pants comic. He is seen
with Ann Corio at left, and in a
scene from the show, below.

113

Early Danny
Danny Thomas looked like this in his burlesque days.

Girl watcher
Hal Skelly, in a burlesque act, ogles the girls over a bulging putty nose.

Lovable imp
Red Buttons (*left*) put his impish smile on display on the burlesque stage.

Joey and Gypsy
Joey Faye is the comic and Gypsy Rose Lee is the nurse in a burlesque scene.

One after another the characters come through—but Lou Costello, as the comic, was a bit surprised one night when Rags Ragland came running through the door, then by his bed, then off the stage. Rags wasn't supposed to be in the scene. Lou was even more surprised when a girl raced through the door behind Rags, waving a real pistol and shouting "Stop, or I'll shoot! You . . . !"

Rags didn't stop, and the girl chased him right up the aisle. The audience roared. A great blackout. The only thing was—it was real. Rags had broken another heart and once again was fleeing for his life.

Mention of Lou Costello is a reminder of those burlesque comics of my day who went on to more lucrative careers.

Of the many is Red Skelton, whose show continues phenomenally year after year in the Top Ten. The TV critics can't understand it, but I do. It's burlesque comedy, and people love it. Red had a great entrance bit. He'd walk on stage, say "Hello, everybody" and keep walking—right into the orchestra pit.

Jackie Gleason started in burlesque, and his greatest success, "The Honeymooners," is really taken from a classic burlesque sketch, "Friendly Neighbors."

Red Buttons' trademark was "Sam, you made the pants too long." He later

won an Academy Award in a picture in which he wore a kimono. So Sam was still at fault.

Professor Lamberti had a funny act. He'd play a xylophone very seriously. But applause would keep breaking out in the wrong spots, right in the middle of his number. He would stop and acknowledge the applause each time graciously. What he didn't know was that a girl was stripteasing behind him, and the applause was for every bit of clothing which floated away. A great act.

Phil Silvers was one of the first Top Bananas not to wear baggy pants and crazy makeup. He did it all verbally with that fast talk, and blinding smile

Rags Ragland, Mr. Private

King—and Clown Prince
Bud Abbott *(left)* and Lou
Costello made up one
of the most popular comedy
teams on the burlesque
stage—and in movies as well.

"Away we go!"
Jackie Gleason got his
start at the Empire
Burlesque Theater
in New Jersey. From
there he traveled far.

of triumph at each small success.

Abbott and Costello met strictly by chance when a producer assigned them to work together. They hit it off right away. Abbott was the perfect straight man; he could maintain his dignity and appeal while pushing chubby Costello around. Some of the sketches they worked up will live forever. "Who's on First?" is revived time and again, but never as well as it was done by Bud and Lou. Another favorite of Costello's was the Schoolroom scene. We do this scene in our show today. It's a corker. Lou played the impish boy who disrupts the class in school, and the audience always screamed when he stood up and said, "I'm a b-a-a-a-a-d boy!"

Mike Sachs, Charlie Robinson, Billy "Cheese 'n' Crackers" Hagan, Steve Mills, Rags Ragland—and Red Skelton, Jackie Gleason, Red Buttons, Professor Lamberti, Phil Silvers, and Abbott and Costello: these were some of the great talents that brought burlesque comedy to new heights in the thirties. In those days there was a saying among men: "I go to burlesque to see the comics!" This statement was always greeted with skeptical laughter, but most of the time it was true. Those comics were great.

Before Sgt. Bilko
Phil Silvers, once a
Top Banana on the
burlesque stage,
reentered a familiar
role when he starred
in the Broadway
show, *Top Banana*.

In the Top Ten
Year after year,
Red Skelton's TV
show rates among the
"Top Ten." And on
television he uses
the same comedy he
learned in burlesque.

The curtain rises

Comic Mac Dennison is the sheik in an Oriental harem

THE CHORUS LINE OF A TYPICAL BUR-lesque show was something to see. They were not by any means the long-limbed beauties that decorated the Ziegfeld show. In fact, they came in all sizes and shapes, some of them pretty weird. What endeared them to burlesque audiences was their zest. They made no pretense at subtlety. From the opening curtain their pitch to the boys was: "Wouldn't you like to meet us?"

Burlesque operators couldn't afford to compete with Broadway shows when it came to chorus girls' salaries. So their shows always ended up with a melange of ingenues just starting out, and vet-erans who had never learned to dance. It made for a pretty funny mixture. But who could quarrel when the girls sang lyrics such as these:

If you love us, please don't mind
If now and then we bump and grind!
We will shimmy and we will shake
But please don't think we're on the make!

"If you love us, please don't mind/if now and then we bump and grind."

When I revived burlesque, I remembered the way real chorus lines used to look in the old days, and I always made sure to have all sorts of girls in the line, not just beauties. I purposely cast one short girl with fat hips, and told her to chew gum and louse up every dance routine. It always broke up the audience.

The reason for the audience's delight is that when the chorus girls came prancing out, with high tinny voices squeaking ridiculous lyrics, they nevertheless thought it was just an ordinary Broadway musical routine. Apparently, most Broadway musicals do the same thing straight. But then the audience would

notice the little fat girl. When the line whirled right, she whirled left. When they danced forward, she tripped back. And she never missed a beat with her bubble gum.

When a sexy chorus girl did a solo routine up front, the little fat girl would crab the act, trying to imitate her, and even

stepping in front of her. Later on I conceived the idea of putting lead in her brassiere. The effect of this was to have the girl's bosom bouncing up and down like a Yo-Yo while she frantically tried to control it.

In a play called *Burlesque* in which Bert Lahr starred, the third act was a burlesque show. I helped Bert prepare this scene, and we used the bumbling chorus-girl bit. The star stripper would go into her act, and the funny chorus girl would be imitating her—but with disastrous results. The stripper kept throwing her clothes on top of the struggling chorus girl. The little girl had to remove two sets of clothing—her own, and the stripper's.

Incidentally, one of the extra jobs of a chorus girl in real life was to be a "catcher." This meant she would stand in the wings, unseen by the audience, and the stripteaser would float her clothes off into space—and the girl would catch them. As I once said to a reporter, "She had to have good hands—like Yogi Berra."

Big name in New York
The Minskys dominated burlesque
for many years, with theatres
that became major showplaces.

Introducing . . .
A red-hot stripper goes into her
act at Minsky's Theater
in Newark. It's a sure thing that
the rafters will be shaking
when she reaches her peak.

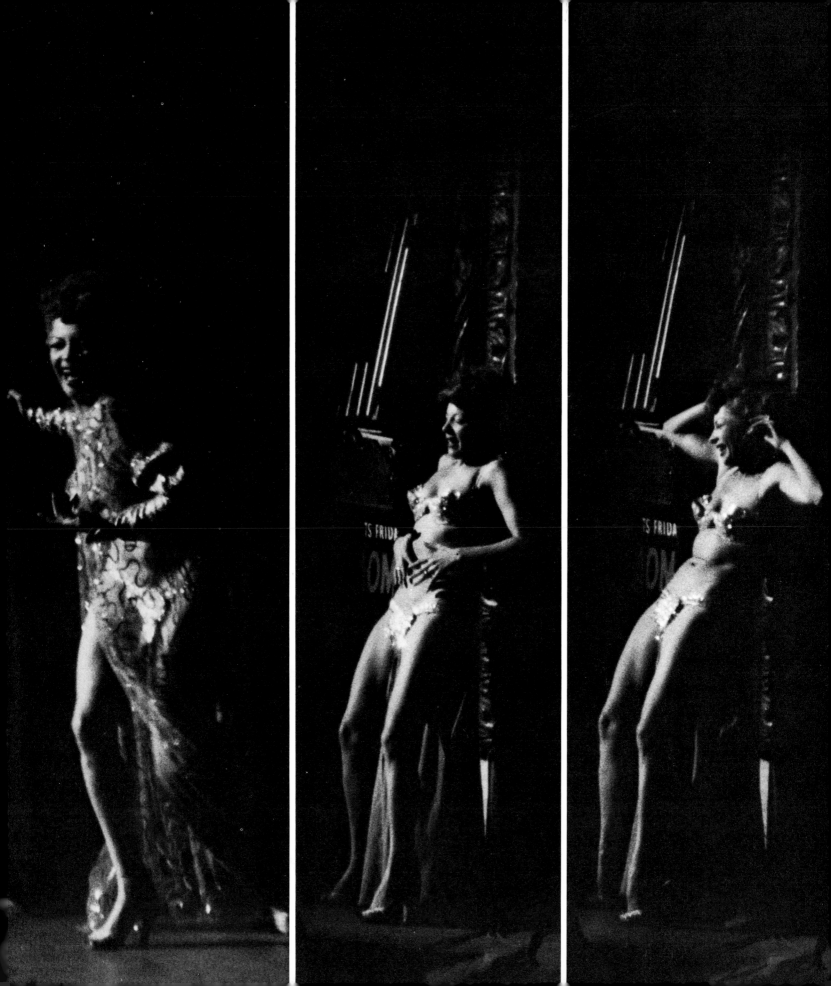

Tenors,
straight men
and
candy butchers

Even tenors
Connie Ryan *(below)*
was one of the best
tenors burlesque ever
had. Dexter Maitland,
working with Steve
Mills as accompanist
at right, also
could hit high C.

COLUMNIST HY GARDNER ONCE WROTE that Robert Merrill, the celebrated Metropolitan baritone, had sung in burlesque. Robert Alda, the star of *Guys and Dolls*, also is one of our alumni. The only thing that I don't understand about these historical items is that both Mr. Merrill and Mr. Alda can sing. This goes counter to the great tradition of burlesque tenors.

For this discussion, I'm sorry that this book is not a record album, because nothing would give me greater pleasure than enclosing a tenor's voice in full falsetto during a typical burlesque number. They would reach for that impossible dream—a high note—and fall back halfway like an exhausted mountain climber.

One of the most nostalgic memories for burlesque fans of the thirties is the striptease star gliding softly through her act while through the microphones came an ear-splitting tenor singing "The Sweetheart of Sigma Chi" or some other inappropriate ballad. Most likely if you asked the stripper what Sigma Chi was she would have told you it was a Rumanian Prince.

But nothing could stop those tenors. For one thing they usually sang in the wings, safe from tomatoes and other thrown objects. For another, they sang with such goodwill, such confidence in themselves, that your eyes told you what your ears would not believe. Any illusions that these fine fellows might have had about their voices were usually shattered by the tough burlesque operators who tolerated them only because it would have been expensive to hire someone who could really sing. The operators put them to work overtime as straight men in different scenes, and got their money's worth.

Connie Ryan is a fine example of the singer–straight man, but he fooled everyone by becoming not only a great straight man but a very good singer. He didn't really have a good voice, but he learned to use his high tenor in such a way that it sounded good. He would team up with a baggy-pants comic such as Steve Mills and do an extraordinary duet, with songs ranging from "Red, Red Robin" to "My Gal Sal."

Connie and Steve opened with our revival in New York, and they brought the house down with their number. It was made particularly effective by the nature of the act. Steve would sing with his gravel-voice bass in counterpoint to Connie's Irish tenor. And he would do

more: he would interject in the middle of a romantic ballad an unexpected funny line. For example, in the song "Sandman" Connie would be singing:

CONNIE: *Mr. Sandman . . .*
STEVE: *Yes?*
CONNIE: *Bring me a dream . . .*
STEVE: *I'll do my best.*
CONNIE: *Make her complexion like peaches and cream . . .*
STEVE: *Oh go to Hell!*

Then, while laughter would ring out, they would finish in a stirring duet:

Mr. Sandman please
Mr. Sandman please
Mr. Sandman please . . . bring me a dream!

Later on Connie became ill, and Paul West joined our show. Paul had one of the sweetest voices ever heard on a stage, a real authentic Irish tenor of the old school. And when Paul and Steve rendered that same act, they got encore after encore. *Life* magazine called them the greatest duet on Broadway.

BURLESQUE COMEDY IS BUILT AROUND two-man teams: the comic and the straight man. Scenes in which the comic played alone in burlesque are rare. Occasionally there would be a musical number in which a comic plays the xylophone, and some performed a comedy striptease. Steve Mills does an excellent comic strip using metal funnels for breasts, which he later moves to his temples so that he looks like an idiot Viking. But almost every other scene depends on the straight men. I have seen, and worked with, many great ones in my time: Dick Dana, Connie Ryan, Paul West, and Bud Abbott.

The straight man was an elegant character, in a seedy way. He wore the right clothes for a gentleman, but somehow they just didn't look right. Compared to the baggy-pants comic, however, he was a tailor's dream. His job was to dominate the comic, to scold him, to get the better of him with the girls, to try to take his money unfairly. When the comic won out, everyone enjoyed his victory.

The straight man also had to be a master of the double-take, which in burlesque and vaudeville is called "the skull."

Perhaps the most famous straight man in the world is Jack Benny, although most audiences think of him as a comic. I don't think he ever played burlesque, but I've never seen a man who could take a comic's gag line, and simply by reacting with a shocked look on his face get a bigger laugh than the comic.

It is said by Benny's biographers that the greatest single laugh he ever received was when a burglar stopped him on a street, and said, "Your money or your life." Benny said absolutely nothing for minutes, and the laughter built and built because the audience knew that skinflint Benny was actually weighing the decision.

The following is an example of a famous burlesque scene, "The Man on the Street," showing a straight man in action. I'm afraid you'll just have to imagine the straight man's visual double-takes and skulls.

STRAIGHT (*enters, walks to center stage*): *Ladies and gentlemen, at this time we present the "Man on the Street" program. My job is to interview different people passing* by. Now if I could secure the services of some young man ... (The comic walks on stage and stands beside straight man. The straight man looks at him.) My friend, I asked for a young man. You'll never live to be as old as you look.

COMIC: No doubt you've heard of the March of Time—this must be his brother, waste of time.

STRAIGHT: Look at the face on that thing. If there is anyone out there with a dog-hunting license—what are you waiting for? My friend, this is the "Man on the Street" program, and I'd like to ask you a few questions. My name is Arliss, and yours?

COMIC: Phillips.

STRAIGHT: Not the Phillips that makes the magnesia?

COMIC: No, the Phillips that takes it.

STRAIGHT: What do you do for a living?

COMIC: I work in a girls' panties factory.

STRAIGHT: Do you make much?

COMIC: I pull down about eighty-five a week.

STRAIGHT: How about your habits. Do you smoke?

COMIC: No, sir.

STRAIGHT: Do you drink?

COMIC: No, sir.

STRAIGHT: Do you go out with women?

COMIC: No, sir.

STRAIGHT: You don't smoke, drink, or go out with women. What do you do for excitement?

COMIC: I throw eggs in electric fans.

STRAIGHT: Did I understand you to say that you don't go out with women?

COMIC: No, they only get you into trouble. I should know, because I've been married eight times. One time I came home unexpected and found my wife in the arms of my best friend. Boy, did I burn up. But what really made me mad was when my wife said, "Honey, pull up a chair and learn something." The same thing happened to a friend of mine who lives down the street from me. But he was a little more ferocious. He came home and found his wife in the arms of his best friend.

STRAIGHT: What did he do?

COMIC: Oh nothing—he just pulled out a butcher knife and stuck it in him.

STRAIGHT: That's terrible. Did he die?

COMIC: Yeah, but it could have been worse.

STRAIGHT: Could have been worse? How?

COMIC: If he had come home a half-hour sooner, he'd a got me!

STRAIGHT: You think that you're smart, don't you?

COMIC: I should be. I was born twins.

STRAIGHT: Born twins? Does that make you smart?

COMIC: Two heads are better than one.

STRAIGHT: Did you have any difficulty with your brother?

COMIC: I should say. Everything he did, I got the blame for it.

STRAIGHT: I don't understand.

COMIC: Well, when we were kids, and played baseball—if he broke a window, I got blamed for it.

STRAIGHT: That's because you looked alike.

COMIC: Yes. If he went into a five-and-ten-cent store and stole something, I got the blame for it.

STRAIGHT: Terrible. What else?

COMIC: Later on in life I met a beautiful girl—and he married her.

STRAIGHT: That's awful.

COMIC: But I got even with him.

STRAIGHT: You got even with him? How?

COMIC: Last week I died—and they buried him!

STRAIGHT: My friend, that about con-cludes the interview, and thanks very kindly for coming up here. However, before you leave, I'd like to inform you that without a doubt you are the most illiterate person that I have ever met.

COMIC: That's right. Build me up.

STRAIGHT: When I say illiterate, I mean that you're dumb. You haven't the intelligence of my youngest child.

COMIC: You have a child? How long have you been married?

STRAIGHT: Three years.

COMIC: That's good. How many children do you have?

STRAIGHT: Six!

COMIC: Married three years, and have six children?

STRAIGHT: Yes.

COMIC: That's damn good! How do you account for having six children, and only being married three years?

STRAIGHT: I attribute it to the reading my wife did.

COMIC: Reading? What's that have to do with it?

STRAIGHT: Well, the first year we were married, my wife read a book entitled One Night of Love, and at the end of that year she presented me with a baby boy. The second year, she read a book entitled A Tale of Two Cities, and at the end of that year she gave birth to twins. The third year, she read a book titled Three Men on a Horse, and at the end of the third year, she presented me with triplets. That makes six altogether. See?

COMIC: Let me get this straight. The first year you were married, your wife read a book called One Night of Love and at the end of the year—bang—there was a baby boy. The second year, she read A Tale of Two Cities and gave birth to twins. The third year,

Playing straight
Dexter Maitland, on
the right, is the
straight man, as Harry
Conley tries to steal
Barbara Rhoades away.

she read Three Men on a Horse *and gave birth to triplets.*

STRAIGHT: *Yes.*

COMIC *(very nervous): I'll see you later—I have to rush home and stop my wife.*

STRAIGHT: *Why?*

COMIC: *She's reading* The Birth of a Nation.

BLACKOUT

OF ALL THE PEOPLE WHO HAVE PASSED into burlesque fame, perhaps the most beloved is the candy butcher. Don't ask me why. This rogue gulled the customers regularly. In a twenty-five-cent candy box he offered them fabulous prizes that turned out to be worthless. At intermission he came out waving books guaranteed to have the spiciest pictures ever seen—and they wouldn't have shocked your grandmother. Still, even today when I announce the candy butcher in our show, there is a ripple of applause and laughter. Everyone loves the candy butcher.

Maybe it was his attitude. It certainly wasn't his English. No one mangled the language more in a desperate effort to push his woebegone products. The candy butcher would appear at the beginning of the show before the curtain rose, and he'd peddle his candy boxes. His spiel would go something like this:

Good evening, ladeez and gentlemen. Tonight we have some fabulous prizes for each and every one of you. A genuwine gold watch,

The candy butcher, still with us

a string of poils, binoculars and opera glasses for those of you with weak eyes ... these are just some of the magnificent prizes you're going to find inside a twenty-five cent box of candy which you will purchase with our guarantee ... each and every box contains a souvenir. You can't lose.

And these aren't presents which you're gonna throw beneath your seat. Nosiree, these are the real thing ... you'll leave this theatre tonight counting your lucky stars because in addition to the best show in the world you're going home a winner ... the recipient of a kind and nice gesture on the part of this here theatre ... a fabulous prize in your pocket nominating you as the smartest guy in the world ... all for the

price of twenty-five cents ... and now turn your attention to the young men passing through the aisles.... There's a winner there ... a gold watch!

He would be pointing to a shill in the audience who would be holding a watch high in the air — no doubt a Mickey Mouse watch, but who knew for sure?

This act was merely the prelude to his climactic performance. During the first intermission, the candy butcher would once again appear on stage. His mission-not-so-impossible? To sell sexy pictures or booklets that were guaranteed to make your hair stand on end. In the thirties, Paris was still considered the sexiest city in the world, and anything French had to be sexy. Consequently, most of these books were peddled as "French." This is the way a typical intermission spiel went:

Ladeez and gentlemen, your attention please for just a few minutes. We have an extra added attraction for you tonight, a chance to buy for your very own one of the most sensational, one of the most spicy, one of the most daring books ever offered at this theatre.

We've been offering books for sale at this theatre before, but never a book like this. No sir, this book will make all those other books look like grade-school kid stuff. They don't compare.

Direct from Paree, France we have received a consignment of books so daring they were banned in gay Paree, and you know what that means. If you don't, let me

explain and describe some of the contents of this book which are guaranteed to keep you up all night reading and dreaming of the charms inside.

The first is the story of a French girl who has been in a convent. A beautiful, love-starved girl with one thing on her mind, ladeez and gentlemen, one thing alone ... and for months she has been shut away inside those granite walls.

But one day she escapes the convent and hitchhikes back to Paree, and I want to explain and elucidate that fact. This is a love-starved girl, shut away in a convent for months, and now she is arriving in Paree and you and I know what Paree means. And who does she meet? An American sailor, a boy who has been on a ship for months. This is the randiest story I personally have ever read ... never will you see such descriptions ... such detail ... such words in a printed book unless you buy this little booklet in my hand. I promise you, it leaves nothing to the imagination; it calls a spade a spade.

Imagine, if you can, what happens when this girl meets this sailor. He goes to her hotel room; she answers the door in a negligee, if you please. Are you beginning to get the picture? This is the real thing. And if this story doesn't make you jump right out of your seat, I advise each and every one of you to see a doctor.

Now here's another little story, each one different, but each one so spicy I cannot tell you all the details right out loud here on the stage. I might get arrested. This story is of a show girl who wants to get into the Folies Bergere. Now this is a gorgeous hunk of girl and she is willing to do anything ... and I meen everything ... to get into that show. And she comes into the office of the producer who is a man who knows his way around the girls . . . he's been producing this show for years . . . and each and every one of you would like to be in his place. And you will be . . . when you're reading this adventure . . . for this girl is determined to get that job, and right now. She locks the office door behind her, and starts taking off her clothes right in his office . . . and you and I can tell there will be fireworks right off. I guarantee you'll get the biggest thrill of your life with this one, and some laughs, too, for this is a producer who thinks he knows everything with a little girl who knows more than he does.

And that's just two of these spicy stories . . . there are eight more, each of them better than the first. And that's not all by any means or a long shot. In the center of this book is the real piece de resistance, which is French for really something! There are pictures of girls as nature intended them to be, as naked as the day they were born, but a lot more fully developed, I guarantee you.

Turn to these pages and you'll come to page nineteen, and I ask you to do that for a very special reason. This is a picture that is so daring you can't even see it in cold print. But it's there all right.

All I ask each and every one of you to do is take this booklet home, turn to page nineteen, turn the book upside down and place the bottom half under the faucet. When that picture gets wet you'll see a sight you didn't believe possible in this day and age . . . a picture so daring it reveals everything and by that I mean everything . . . not just a nude picture . . . not a pin-up . . . no sir, this is a picture that will send you through the ceiling.

Those books would sell so fast the boys in the back row would miss their chance. And were *they* lucky? Because as a candy butcher told me backstage one day, "When those boys put that picture under the faucet, you know what they're going to have? . . . The wettest hand in town."

First Act Finale—and time for the candy butcher

Backstage at burlesque

LET ME TAKE YOU BACKSTAGE AT A TYPI-cal burlesque show in the thirties. I advise you to hold your hat — over your eyes.

With the possible exception of the Ringling Bros. Circus I can't imagine any scene more colorful than the backstage area of a burlesque show. For one thing the comics worked in a number of different costumes, ranging from baggy pants to white-tie and tails. For another the props were ridiculous; wooden pop guns, seltzer bottles, hog bladders, chamber pots, policeman's pistols, and girl's panties.

How that last prop works in an act may be illustrated in a famous panto-mime scene. I played it with Charlie Robinson, one of the all-time great pantomimists. In the sketch Charlie was a drunk on the verge of passing out in a bar, and I was a girl determined to steal his wallet. Drunk as he was, he always foiled my efforts — and each time just at the most unexpected moment. The audience roared. Finally I succeeded. I had his wallet. I held it in the air to show the audience. Charlie looked up at me and shrugged. Then he showed the audience what *he* had pickpocketed from me — and pulled out of his coat a pair of panties.

Chaos always reigned backstage at burlesque. In addition to comics tearing

Behind the scenes
Backstage burlesque intrigued American artist Stuyvesant Van Veen, who painted this casual dressing-room scene.

136

to and fro to make costume changes, there were scads of girls in various stages of undress. Most of the time they were in a hurry, too; and they would emerge from the dressing room pell-mell, only half-dressed. There they would be in the wings, chattering away, perhaps completely naked on top while they finished dressing. Sometimes I wonder how stagehands had the nerve to ask to get paid at a burlesque show. What happened is only natural. The stagehands usually fell in love with the girls. How could they not, when night after night they were treated to a sight that only a husband should see. And if the stagehand was at all attractive he reaped rewards that never appear in a union contract.

Beautiful girls, half-naked; tenors trying out a few notes; strippers in queenlike regalia; comics in crazy hats and tattered rags, and pants that sagged—this was the backstage scene. Steve Mills's pants sagged so badly up front, by the way, that one time the straight man on an impulse pulled the front of his pants even farther away from his body and looked down into the void. After a moment, he said, "I see you got a new pair of shoes!" Steve, as usual, was up to the occasion. He looked down into the same void, and said, sorrow-

A stripper pauses before going on

Harry Conley laughs it up with the chorus girls

Marilyn Simon, forever blowing bubbles

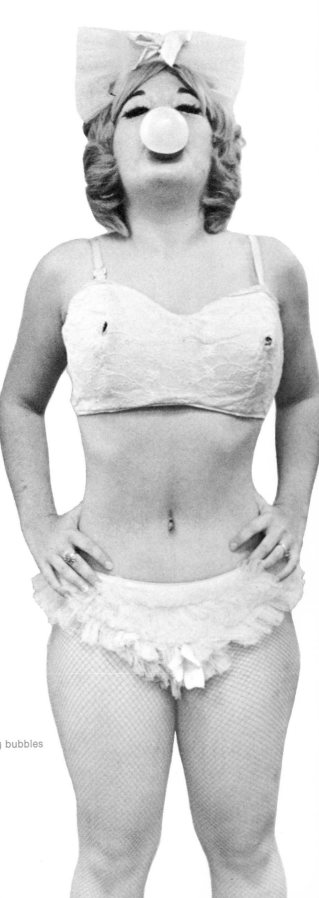

fully, "Hello, there, Green Giant! What's new besides 'Ho ho ho!'"

When we had a truly funny character we had even more fun. For example, there was a stripteaser named Dolores Du Vaughan, who was the darling of the cast. Reason? She believed anything we told her. For example, the stagehands told her—and she believed them—that there was a man living in the flies high above us. What's more, the man had gotten word to us that he was in love with Dolores. This piqued Dolores' curiosity and for the next several days we spotted her looking longingly up into the darkness wonder-

ing who her unknown lover was. Then the stagehands gave Dolores some bad news. Her lover up in the flies had caught a fever. He was dying. Day after day they gave her gloomy medical reports, as the fever soared and soared. It was touching. Dolores was so overcome with worry she could hardly take her clothes off.

The reason for the so-called fever was that the crew had discovered a coffin in the basement, which had been used for a previous legitimate show. One day Dolores arrived backstage to find a funeral in progress. Her lover had died. His body had been taken to be cremated,

and all that was left in the coffin was a handkerchief with his pathetic belongings, and a sealed envelope for Dolores. That envelope contained one of the greatest love notes ever written. It told of a man, doomed to spend his life in the flies of a theatre, who at last sees his true love beneath him, how he had yearned for her from afar—and dreamed of the day when he could take her up into the flies with him. Dolores wept real tears that night. After all these years she had met a really sincere man, and now—as one of the stagehands cruelly put it—he had made an ash of himself.

Jerry Lester has a way with a maid, Carol Peterson

Waiting for the next number

The
feeling
is
mutual

THE WHEEL OF FORTUNE WAS SPINNING, and in the heyday of burlesque, which we now entered, that Wheel was Mutual. It spun us across the country to different cities, bringing laughs and naughtiness wherever it went, and always on schedule.

Today, the Mutual Wheel has long since gone, but in my mind I can still see those train stations, with the huge locomotives huffing and puffing along the platform, and the colorful burlesque troupes arriving to journey to another town. Each show would have special cars for the troupe, and as you walked toward the train you'd see a sign: "ANN CORIO COMPANY, *Track 12*."

It was quite a company. Most people may imagine a burlesque company to consist only of a few strippers, a couple of comics, and a straight man; but in the days of the Mutual Wheel, a burlesque company was as big – or bigger – than most touring Broadway musicals of today. This was a typical company of the day: a striptease star, a prima donna, a soubrette, a talking woman, a boy and girl dance team, two comics, a straight man, a singing juvenile, twelve or fourteen chorus girls, a musical conductor, three stage hands, and an assortment of cats, dogs, monkeys, etc. (the actors' pets). In other words, a minimum of twenty-six people – plus all of the scenery and props.

We were a familiar sight on the railroads for years, as the Wheel kept turning. It was a Wheel with a northern star, Boston; a western frontier, St. Louis; a southern Cross, Washington; and an eastern horizon in towns like Baltimore, Philadelphia, and Newark.

I loved the Wheel. I never played New York much. I found the money was greener out in the pastures. It was steady money, because of the Wheel. What touring Broadway show of today wouldn't like to have forty weeks a year guaranteed? We had fun, too, and we met some great characters. I'd like to tell you some of my experiences on the Wheel in those funny days, and let you meet a few of the people who were always on the burlesque scene.

The St. Louis theatre we played in was the Garrick. It featured a most unusual piano player in the orchestra pit. His Honor, Judge Reidelberger. Why a judge played a piano in a burlesque house I'll never know. Maybe he was just following the precedent set by one of the most famous judges of all, Oliver Wendell Holmes, of the Supreme Court.

Justice Holmes came to see me many times at another famous stop on the Mutual Wheel, the Gayety Theatre in Washington. Perhaps no other burlesque theatre in America had as many celebrated visitors as this little theatre. Jimmy Lake, the proprietor, was probably the most famous operator in the business. In Washington he was a friend of great statesmen, and a symbol of a colorful side of the Capitol. Let's face it, Washington can be the dullest city in the country, when it is not waging war. All of the fun in Washington for a long time was to be found on shabby Ninth Street, and Jimmy with his lively theatre and saloon next door provided most of the laughs.

In those days Drew Pearson called me "the pet of the diplomatic circle." He complained that a red-blooded American boy couldn't get a date with me, because of the foreign competition. Not long after that, President Roosevelt called Drew "a congenital liar," but I'll back him up all the way.

Of course, the most famous customer of the Gayety was Oliver Wendell Holmes. Holmes loved burlesque. It was the Judge who said, while laughing at a burlesque scene, "Thank God I am a man of low taste."

Speaking of low taste reminds me of an experience on another link in the Mutual chain: Columbus, Ohio.

Gayety plus
Girls stand on pedestals on the stage of the Gayety in Washington. This burlesque theatre was one of the key stops on the Mutual Wheel.

Columbus is one of the nicer Midwestern cities, comparatively clean, with lovely residential areas surrounding it. But, as you might expect, one could find a kook among its citizens as well as among those of any other city. I certainly did.

I had an impacted wisdom tooth that caused me pain all during the matinee performance. Immediately after that show I went to a dentist someone had recommended to me. What a scene! I came into the dentist's office worrying only about the pain in my jaw, and found the good Doctor staring at me. "Your lipstick," he said. "It's beautiful!" Then he added, reverently, "*Mary* would like that."

Who was Mary? His wife? I couldn't have cared less. All I wanted was a tooth removed. Instead, he placed me in his chair, stared at me from six inches away, and said: "Those eyes. They're gorgeous. Mary would like them, too."

By now he had my jaw jammed with cotton wads, so—even if I were that vulgar—I couldn't say what I felt with all my heart about him or Mary.

He busily began to treat the tooth, all the time remarking about various features of my beauty that he admired. I tell you, if you want real thrills, try having your tooth pulled by a sex

Margie Hart opens their eyes

maniac — especially one who keeps saying: "Mary would like that!"

By the time he finished I was groggy, nervous, and scared, more or less in that order. But he wouldn't let me go. Oh no. Not until I met . . . Mary. "You mean she's here?" I asked.

"Of course. In the next room."

I have to admit by now I was rather curious to meet this Mary — who would like everything about me. So I accompanied the dentist into a private room off the office. It was dark, and the dentist turned on the lights — and standing there was a *life-size doll*. Mary! I jumped eighteen feet without moving. Then I fled the dentist, and his true love.

Incidentally, it occurred to me that Mary must have given the dentist a chance for some funny conversations with his friends. I can just hear some of his male companions asking who Mary was, and his replying, "She's a doll!" If they only *knew*.

The Cleveland theatre of the Mutual Wheel, the Roxy, I remember as one of my rare financial triumphs — that is, it was in this theatre that I took a financial gamble and won, for a change. My salary had been climbing and climbing and when it reached $1,500 a week, the Roxy owner, George Young, started playing the theatre owner's favorite

Hitting the road
A burlesque troupe used to take to the road by railway. Ann Corio and company now travel by air.

tune: poor mouth. He said business was so bad in his town he just couldn't afford $1,500. So I startled him with a counter offer. I'd work for $300 a week, but with a percentage of the gross, 25% to be exact. That percentage sounds high, and you may be surprised that George agreed to it. The reason is simple. Most performers, while on stage, are far from the box office. All performers with a percentage of the gross at one time or another have stared out at a packed house, only to have the manager claim after the show that it was only a third full. He would produce a batch

of tickets claiming these were all he sold. What did I do to counter this threat to my financial solidity? I brought in my own manager to count the tickets. Then I put on the show on a "grind basis," perhaps never seen before — *seven* shows a day, as distinct from the usual *four*.

All of a sudden Mr. Young realized he had made a colossal gaffe. Show after show was packed — and I was to get 25%. In the middle of the week, he returned to my dressing room pleading with me to accept the original $1,500. But a deal is a deal. After paying off

Reginald Marsh's painting, "The Star Theater"

148

everyone, the performers who worked overtime, the manager who counted the tickets, I cleared nearly $10,000 for myself in that week. Good old Cleveland! Good old George Young!

In Dayton, another stop on the Wheel, one of my vivid memories is of the musical conductor. He played the violin, and he also played the G-string.

Our prima donna was in love with this sentimental violinist. The poor girl couldn't contain herself. She would stand in the wings during the performance staring into the eyes of her lover in the pit and suddenly break into song. This went over big in the middle of a comedy scene.

Their favorite song was "Clair de Lune." What else? I found this out to my sorrow one day when I was right in the middle of my number. My own song was, and is, "A Pretty Girl is Like a Melody." I was gliding through my act almost absentmindedly when suddenly I tripped! The love-struck conductor, catching sight of his girl in the wings, had switched the orchestra to their song, "Clair de Lune." I gave him a "ten-pound" look, but it did no good at all. He was sawing away, his eyes only on his true love. Who said burlesque wasn't romantic? After that performance I wanted to take a bow and wrap it around the violinist's neck.

Philadelphia was a major stop on the Wheel. In fact, it had two theatres, the Troc and the Shubert. Next to Boston, Philadelphia was perhaps my favorite town, as far as loyal fans are concerned. Occasionally I would play in Philadelphia for weeks at a time—but always at the Shubert. I didn't care for the Troc because they worked too "strong" there.

My buddy Lou Costello, then the number one movie star, would come down to Philly to see me sometimes. He was always playing practical jokes on me ranging from fake phone calls from Cecil B. DeMille to drawing a skull and crossbones on my dressing room mirror with an eyebrow pencil. That's why I immediately thought of Lou when I received a threatening note in Philadelphia one day. For one thing, Lou was coming down that evening. When he arrived I showed him the threatening note. It said: "We want $5,000 in small bills. Do not notify the police. We know your family lives in Hartford."

Now that was a scary note—and certainly a lousy joke. I gave Lou the devil when he came into my dressing room. But he had a surprise for me: he hadn't written the note.

I was stunned. For the first time, I realized this was serious. Someone was threatening to do harm to my family. I called my mother immediately and told her to come to Philadelphia. I figured she'd be safer with me, especially as my next move was to notify the FBI.

Every day I'd wait for a phone call at my hotel. For two days, nothing happened. Then on the third day the phone rang, and this gruff-voiced person asked me if I was going to comply with their demands. I said yes, especially as I knew that the FBI was on the line, listening in. He said he'd call me back and arrange the contact. He was not what I call the brightest blackmailer. The place he chose to receive the money was not a lonely farm on a moonless night, but the stage door of the Shubert. Maybe he thought the normal confusion and crowds there would help him escape. I don't know. But my heart was beating fast when I had to keep that rendezvous. Maybe he was a maniac who would plunge a knife into me—or throw acid—or do something crazy.

In the movies or television, usually when a gangster is going to contact a victim, near the location of the contact are a street cleaner and a delivery boy—both of them, FBI men. That was exactly the situation at my rendezvous with

the blackmailer. I went to the stage door but immediately had a problem. One of those characters who hang around burlesque theatres (and other theatres, too) just to share some of the glamor was in the way. I'd seen this particular creep for years; he was part of the scenery. I looked over his shoulder impatiently, hoping he'd leave so we could get a clear shot at the criminal. Then this character whispered, "Where's the money?" I almost dropped my bra! He was the blackmailer.

My own Elliot Nesses moved in fast and carried him off for safekeeping. All of a sudden, just like that, it was over. I don't mind telling you my knees were playing a tune called "you coward, you!" They composed it themselves.

That all happened in Philadelphia. And that's why I'm the only one in any group who laughs whenever comics say Philadelphia is dull.

In addition to the stops on the Wheel, burlesque shows played other towns, too, sometimes on a series of one-nighters, hopping across the country by bus. That was gruelling work then, and it is today. As I was the star I had in my own contract a provision for first-class transportation. That clause meant I could take a sleeping car between stops, while the rest of the poor cast traveled in an old broken-down bus.

One person in our troupe, the musical

Spirit of '76
Burlesque has always used every prop it could find—including the good old American flag.

conductor, never stopped complaining. It wasn't fair, he argued. How could I look the rest of the company in the face when I would arrive in a town, fresh as new linen, while the sleepless company bumped in on an old bus. Finally, I couldn't take it any longer. I said to him one night,"OK, you take the sleeper tonight. I'll go by bus."

"You're a queen!" he said, and I had a new friend. That night I climbed on the bus with the rest of the gang, and we started rolling out of town on a dark night. Suddenly, about ten miles out of town, we had to stop. There was a train wreck ahead—and you know who was on the train.

The next morning a very bitter man arrived just in time for the show. He was our musical conductor, although it was hard to tell because he looked like a mummy. I never did convince him that I didn't plan that train wreck. And no one else ever asked for my ticket.

And so the Mutual Wheel spun, with laughs and money all the way round for burlesquers in the thirties. I must pause now for my favorite stop of all. It was in Boston, of all places, home of the original Puritans, teeming with Watch and Ward Societies and Blue Laws. But it was also the home of my favorite theatre, the Old Howard, and my favorite audience, the Harvard student body.

You can't graduate until you've seen Ann Corio

THERE NEVER WAS A THEATRE LIKE THE Old Howard. For one thing, it was a burlesque theatre that resembled a *church*. It was built that way on purpose because when it opened, on October 13, 1845, the good citizens of Boston considered a theatre an instrument of the devil. The canny builders of the Old Howard fooled them by building a great, gray, Gothic edifice complete with three tall, stained-glass windows in the front. In addition, they called it, not the Old Howard theatre, but the Howard Athenaeum.

Inside, the Old Howard was built like an ancient Greek theatre, with a circle apron, and the audience on three sides. Boxes ranged up from the sides in tiers, and those boxes more often than not were filled with the greater part of the Harvard student body.

The Old Howard was my favorite theatre, and my favorite audience was from the educational institution along the Charles River. Friday's midnight performance was Harvard's show of shows. How those boys would howl. They took possession of me. I was their girl, and around the circuit, wherever there were other colleges, I was known as "Harvard's baby."

I used to have a gag I'd pull at that Friday midnight show. I'd start my number the same way as always, but gradually I'd be edging closer and closer to the side of the stage where all the boxes were filled with Harvard students. When I was pretty nearly undressed there by the side of the stage, I'd suddenly have the spotlight thrown on the upper boxes. And there would be the Harvard boys hanging by their toes to get a good look at my bosom.

I had fans in the faculty, too. An astronomy professor asked his class to name a heavenly body. One student yelled out, "Ann Corio." An anthropology teacher, Professor Hooten, asked me to visit his home and have tea with the family. Professor Hooten had a sense of humor in his own right. I could tell when I met one of his sons and heard the name his parents had given him. Newton. Full name: Newton Hooten.

There I was, having tea, if you please, with an academic great. We discussed anthropology. Did I think beauty was hereditary? Was it inherited from ones' parents? I answered these and other questions for a while, and then I asked *him* a question. "Professor, how can you explain the great amount of deafness in Boston?"

"Deafness? I didn't know we had an excessive amount."

I said there must be, because night

Period playbills
Programs from the Old Howard show the early dominance of vaudeville, and the start of its replacement by burlesque.

The Big Continuous Stage Show
AT THE HOWARD THIS WEEK.
Each Act will be Designated by Card Displayed on the Stage

THE HOWARD OLIO.
BOWERY BURLESQUERS.
Olio.

AL. LEACH and the THREE ROSEBUDS,
In the funny sketch, " Examination Day at School."

JAMES RICHARD GLENROY, The man with the green gloves.	BILLY and FRANKIE WILLIAM " Lindy and the Lady."
SAM and IDA KELLY, Comedy Sketch.	MR. and MRS LARRY SHAW Comedy Act.
EDWIN and KITTIE DEAGON, In a Novelty Sketch.	BILLY HINES.

The Howard Comedy Co., in a New Farce

CHAS. BURNHAM, ANNIE CARTER,	JOHN S. PHILLIPS. MAUD CAMPBEL.
NACIREMA TWIN MIDGETS, Songs and Acrobatic Dancing.	GILBERT and GOLDIE, Comedy Entertainers.

Wait for the beautiful Indian Princess-Yutakmee. | **Wait for the beautiful Indian Princess-Yutakm**

NEVA AMAR assisted by BEN JANSEN, Empress of Negro melodies.	TAYLOR TRIO—Frank Taylor, Et Cope & Tom Carter—Return of the min

The Leading Ladies, HENSHAW, FRANCIOLA & CO., In a trial in vaudeville. By Mark Bennett, of Bennett and Rich.	Wait for the beautiful Indian Princess-Yutakmee. Frank—HAYES & SUITS—Anna Singing and Dancing Specialty.

Concluding with the original burletta, entitled

"SLUMMING."

(Booked by Loney Haskell. A satire on the latest N. Y. craze, introducing all newest fads,) Staged by Andy Lewis. Costumes designed by Will R. Barnes, of London, Paris and Australia.
Cast of characters by the company.

Special Feature.—YUTAKMEE, the beautiful Indian Princess.
During the action of the travesty on "Slumming," the following musical numbers will be introduced :

Scene 1—Opening chorus by the entire company. Waitress Song, Misses Robinson, Lewis. Ware, Dumont. Red Soubrette—Mignon Gilbert, "Good-morning, Carrie." May Irwin—Neva Aymar, ' Go 'Way Back and Sit Down." Pete Dailey—Walter Goldie. "Manola, Lady Hottentot." Pauline Hall—Virgie Ware, "Lullaby" from "Erminie." Anna Held—Mignon Gilbert, "Oh, Won't You Come and Play With Me." Military Final—Misses, Cope, Sulis and Company. "He Laid Away the Suit of Gray." Scene 2—"Mamie," Frank Taylor and Georgie Franciola. "Polly," Frank Hays, Mabel Brown, and Misses Robinson, Golden, Clayton, Lewis, Ware, Harri-, Wells, and Gordon. Scene 3—Doraflora Octette, Misses Brown, Wells, Lewis, Ware, Harri-a, Clayton, Golden and Dumont. "I Must Have Been Dreaming," and Medley of Popular ngs, by the entire company. Hebrew Parody, Wm. Gilbert and Ben Janson. YUTAKMEE ndian Princess. Final, "My Dusky Bride," by the entire company.
Time—Present. Place—New York.

First Scene—Bowery Concert Hall.   Second scene—Chinatown.
Third scene—Grand ballroom of Waldorf Astoria.

THIS WEEK CONTINUED.

THE KINETOGRAPH
A Moving Picture Sensation

The Merry Burlesque, entitled

"STAND PAT"
REPRESENTED BY

GLADYS EISHER	MAZIE YALE	KITTIE HARTFORD
ROSE CARLIN	CARRIE MACK	JULIA HEINTZMAN
LILLIAN TAYLOR	ALLIE VIVIAN	MAY BELMONT
JULIA CROSBY	MARIE REVERE	KATE REVERE
IDA MANTELL	NELLIE HARTFORD	

THE BUNCH

Claire Romaire	Jennie Innes	Edith Meredith
Esther Maitland	Josephine Bonete	Dorothy Moore
Belle Thursby	Grace Manchester	Lily Mason
Clara Coady	Charlotte Clarke	Anna Bigler
Anna Waltman	Marie Kent	Emma Russell
Stella Drew	Amy Stone	Laura Leicester
Pearl Irving	May Hamilton	Lizzie Kelly
Florence Carleton	May Bennett	Mabel Cleveland

Produced under the Personal Direction of
MISS VIOLET MASCOTTE

AT THE OLD HOWARD

WAIT AND HEAR
Mae Taylor Sing
This Week.

The Big Continuous Stage Show
AT THE HOWARD THIS WEEK.
Each Act will be Designated by Card Displayed on the Stage

WATERBURY BROS. and TENNEY
In the Musical Comedy, " A Cold Day in July "

BAKER and LYNN Presenting " The Electric Boy"	CLEMENSO BROS. Musical Clowns
HARPER, DESMOND, and BAILEY The Three Black Diamonds	RASTUS and BANKS The Major and the Maid
Chas.—GREGSONS—Flora In their Novel Sketch "A 16th Century Courtship"	MILLARD BROS. Banjoists, Dancers, Singers
HOWLEY and LESLIE Singing and Dancing Duo	HAYMAN and FRANKLIN Presenting "A Matrimonial Agency "
GRACIE and REYNOLDS Irish Comedy Sketch Artists	MURRAY and SILVA Comedy Sketch
MUSICAL HOLBROOKS Musical Novelties	AL. CHRISTAL Singing Comedian

WESTON SISTERS
Songs and Dances and Burlesque Boxing

(Program Continued on Page 6.)

after night hundreds of people at the Old Howard asked for front-row seats. They claimed to be "hard of hearing."

The slogan at the Old Howard became famous throughout New England. "Always Something Doing from 9 A.M. to 11 P.M." This was especially true when the fabulous Jim Curley was Mayor. I don't think I ever played a week at the Old Howard without at least one ceremonial visit from Jim Curley, his wife, and loyal staff. And what a production they would make of their entrance! They wouldn't reserve seats ahead of time. They didn't need to. The show would be underway and suddenly I'd spot a commotion in the back of the theatre. Down the aisles would come ushers with folding chairs, and set them up right in front of the stage in the aisle space. Then, the Mayor and his retinue would roll down the aisle for a glimpse of burlesque heaven.

He was a wonderful, colorful mayor, and Boston loved him. I did, too. Today politicians seem to come out of computers, and theatres have no personality of their own; but when Jim Curley was in his heyday, and the Old Howard was brightening things up, life was always interesting—from 9 A.M. to 11 P.M.

I don't know if there are ghosts in Boston. But if there are, some of them must surely be visiting the site where the Old Howard stood, and shedding an invisible tear. Those ghosts would not all be from burlesque, for the performers who trod the Old Howard stage included not only myself, Margie Hart, and the other strippers—but Edwin Booth, Sarah Bernhardt, and many other of the greatest actors and actresses of all time. The Old Howard, long before we got there, was dedicated to legitimate theatre. Its first production was Sheridan's *School for Scandal*, and in the following thirty years all four of the Booth brothers, and Madam Sarah, played in one production or another.

By 1870, however, interest in the legitimate drama was on the wane, and the Old Howard shifted its main bill of fare to melodrama and variety shows. Acrobats, magicians, jugglers, and dancers kept the theatre busy. The daily, special attractions were exhibitions of prizefight champions, the most popular of all being John L. Sullivan.

During this period the Athenaeum became known as the Old Howard. But its most exciting years were yet to come. Around 1900 one of Boston's top showmen, Dr. G. E. Lothrop, took over control of the theatre and instituted a policy of burlesque.

By the time I arrived in the thirties, the Old Howard was a legend. But the press agents were still as effusive. Here's the way I was billed before one of my appearances:

When we slide you the heated vapor that Ann Corio trips here at the Old Howard, we've tooted something worthwhile to every regular scout. The most beautiful girl on the stage will give the wisenheimers a merry marathon. Here comes the peachiest peach in the game, and the babe with the perpetual smile will deliver the material that gathers the glances from pit to dome.

By that time the theatre was owned by Al Somerby, one of the most respected operators in the business. He kept a firm hand on his shows, and during his time of ownership the need for censorship was slight.

We never got tired of exploring the Old Howard. There were all kinds of rumors about it, perhaps springing from its church-like appearance, which gave every burlesquer a surprise when he first arrived.

One story is that it actually was a church at one time. A Mr. Miller had a flock called the "Millerites." He predicted the end of the world for a certain day. The flock gathered with him on the appointed Day and waited for the Pearly Gates to open. When darkness came—and no Pearly Gates—Mr. Miller's flock flew away.

Miner and Van's offering in 1891

156

A SCRAMBLED EGG.

The Performance to conclude with a Roaring One Act Comedy, entitled

Something borrowed, something new,
And much that's funny to please you.

The Home of Comedy, Vaudeville and Burlesque

PROGRAMME

Matinee at 2.15.   Week of Mar. 20, '99.   Evenings at 8.

OVERTURE .... ORCHESTR

MINER and VAN'S

Bohemian Burlesquers.

MINER and VAN, Proprietors.

Frank—FISHER and JANSEN—Flo
Original Acrobatic and Comedy Artists.

Chas.—SAXON and BROOKS—Florence
Rendering Gems of Opera and Songs Illustrated.

PROGRAMME CONTINUED.

CAST.

Patsy Bolivar, a bell-boy at Hotel Bohemia	BILLY B. VAN
Jay Hasben, landlord at Hotel Bohemia	Frank Evans
Sample Slick, a patent medicine drummer	Charles Saxon
Col. Con Greenbox, manager of the Burlesquers	Will A. Vidocq
Shakespeare Shake-to-death, a "legit"	
Wayback Johnson, the town constable	Frank Fisher
Eli Evergreen, an eager bridegroom	
Airy Harry, only a dude	
Blankety Blanco, a bad Spaiard	Alfred Harster
Rev. Obadiah, Too Good, the village Pastor	Charles Saxon
Carrots, chamber maid at Hotel Bohemia	VEVIE NOBRIGA
Millie Tiptoe, the traditional gay soubrette	Myrtle Tressider
Symanthy Simpkins, a giddy old girl	Florence Brooks
Sadie Slob, a blushing bride	Vera Belle
Vera Sweet	Emma Watson
Pinkey Sweet	Celebrated	Flo Janson
Trickey Sweet	Sweet Sisters,	Phylis Price
Osa Sweet	Dora Denton
Gertie Rush	Jennie Russell
Mamie Hush	Calice Reto
Maggie Blush	Mabel Rivers
Cannie Rush	Florence Wade
Sophie Crush	Carrie May
Fannie Slush	Katherine Havron
Sadie You Lush	Sadie Wilson

SCENE—Office of the Hotel Bohemia, Manasquan, N. J.   TIME—Yesterday, to-day or to-morrow.

PROGRAMME CONTINUED,

Frank—EVANS and VIDOCQ—Will
Talking Comedians.

Billy B.—VAN and NOBRIGA—Vevie
And their Komedy Koons.

MYRTLE TRESSIDER
The Girl of '99·
Assisted by ROBBIE NORTH, Phenomenal Newsboy Tenor.

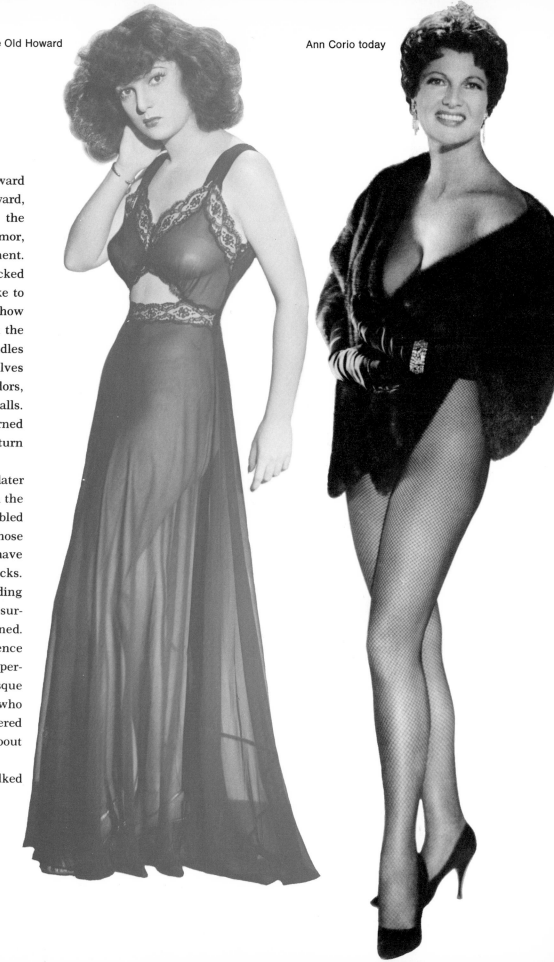

Ann Corio at the Old Howard

Ann Corio today

Another story was that the Old Howard had been built on top of a graveyard, and there were ghosts extant in the building. To add to this happy rumor, there were catacombs in the basement. Mr. Somerby kept the basement locked from the performers who might like to explore. But before one midnight show I and some other brave souls from the cast went down there. We lighted candles in the pitch dark and found ourselves walking down ghostly cell-like corridors, with strange markings on the walls. It was spooky—so spooky that we turned back in a hurry and never to return again.

Some stagehands a few years later were not so lucky. They went up in the flies to do a repair job, and stumbled over a row of coffins. If one of those coffin lids had moved, we would have had three stagehands with heart attacks.

Meanwhile, on stage, I was building my own loyal cult of fans, and a surprising thing—for those days—happened. The wives of the men in the audience said they wanted to come to see me perform. In the thirties a girl in a burlesque audience was a rarity indeed, one who was stared at and who others considered a fallen woman—or, at least, one about to fall.

The manager came to me and talked

158

about this strange phenomenon, and together we came up with a unique idea, one that, to my knowledge, was never tried before or since in a burlesque theatre. Not only would we let ladies into the theatre, but we would hold a special Ladies' Night—women only. That show was a complete sell-out, and the publicity was tremendous. I had struck new pay dirt, and I went right to Mr. Somerby and requested a Ladies' Night every week. But Mr. Somerby said no. When I cried, "Why not?" he answered with indisputable logic, "We don't have a ladies' room."

Nevertheless, even with the plumbing difficulties, I always had lots of women in my audiences whenever I came to Boston. This trend continued to the present day. Recently *Life* magazine sent a reporter to interview me at our show. He was stunned to see busloads of women arriving for each performance. When the magazine came out, his article was titled, "Women Discover Burleycue." Actually, they had discovered it twenty years before, at the Old Howard.

Those were happy days for me; I always felt I was "coming home" when I played the Old Howard, the theatre known as the "wicked old lady of Scollay Square." The Old Howard played on and on, long after I left burlesque. But

Mr. Somerby left the scene, and more daring operators took over. Their boldness led to the end.

Rose La Rose had made herself a reputation as "the bad girl of burlesque" because of her uninhibited actions on stage. In 1953 detectives slipped by the censor-guard with cameras concealed in their coats. Through the button holes of their coats they shot infra-red film of Rose La Rose's dance. That film, when shown in court, resulted in the closing of the Old Howard to burlesque forever.

Boston, however, had by then taken the Old Howard to its heart. In 1959 the Howard National Theater and Museum Committee was organized to save the theatre from threatened demolition. I was an active member of the group. The Committee wanted to convert the Old Howard into a national theatre shrine where operas and plays could be presented.

In 1961 I arrived in Boston with the first edition of our show, *This Was Burlesque*. We were going to try it out in a nightclub in the vicinity. I hastened right over to pay a visit to my beloved Old Howard, even though it was empty. Then, a few weeks later, a mysterious fire started in the theatre and swept murderously through the whole interior. Only the charred outside shell

Unblushing Rose
Rose La Rose on stage was more than a bit risqué. One day a censor smuggled a camera into the theatre, and that ended the Old Howard.

remained standing. I went there right after the fire and looked brokenhearted at the ruins. Then I saw an amazing sight. It was as if that old burnt-down theatre was saying a personal goodbye to the one star on hand for the funeral. The raging fire had burned through layers and layers of posters on its walls— all the way through to a poster put up twenty years before. That poster was of me.

But I didn't have long to brood. Within hours, a city wrecking crew moved in and demolished the granite walls. They hardly waited for the fire to cool. And then a much hotter fire started; this time in the columns of the theatre critics. All of them realized too late that a great institution had been destroyed.

Robert Taylor, the critic of the *Boston Herald*, wrote that the Old Howard's exit "was as spectacular as a Viking's funeral; a curtain in the grand manner." But then this theatre was always grand; and, as Taylor wrote, "Every gesture the playhouse ever contrived had charm." In this obituary for a unique building, the critic quoted me as calling the Old Howard a "valentine."

She was right, of course. It had the fragile and pastel style of a place dedicated to the essentials of the stage. Not a building designed to allow the ultimate in sight lines, to enable players to be heard better, to permit the manipulation of sets, but to create illusion. When you walked into the Old Howard you were not substituting the environment of one part of prosaic everyday life for another; you were in a theatre. And with all its illusion and enchantment.

Mr. Taylor concluded his memorial with these words:

. . . the theatre of the Booths and of the clowns and strippers has burned, and it is never a happy occasion when a theatre dies, even as a ghost of itself. The memories survive, and they are as immortal as stage memories can be. We shall sing no sad songs for, while it lasted, there was always something doing at the Howard Athenaeum from 9 A.M. to 11 P.M.

Last goodbye
Ann Corio was tearful when this picture was taken. The Old Howard had burned— and only her poster remained.

161

The all-time classic comedy scenes

The Courtroom

No Courtroom scene, as such, exists; but out of the Courtroom situation dozens and dozens of versions have evolved. Burlesque comics speak of the Courtroom scene as "Hagan's version," "Smith's version," "Costello's version," etc. And now Sammy Davis has made Pigmeat Markham's version famous— and every teenager in America is shouting, "Heah cum de Judge."

The hero of the Courtroom is a demented Judge, who has an eye for the ladies. In fact, this eye sometimes wanders to ankle-level, as the respected Judge opens a little door at the bottom of his desk and peeks out at the pretty witness.

The Judge is armed with a weapon that you can't find anymore: the bladder. In the old days burlesque comics would go to the neighborhood slaughterhouse and buy a pig's bladder. This would then be dried and inflated. The bladder was needed because the running motif of the Courtroom was the Judge flailing away at the heads of the prosecuting attorney, the defense counsel, and the crazy cop in attendance. What the bladder did was make a terrific crack, without hurting anyone.

When This Was Burlesque opened we scurried around to get such a bladder and found out that in modern-day slaughterhouse operations, these bladders are no longer available. Maybe they grind them up for children's cereal, or turn them into penicillin, or whatever. But they're not available for conking a defense counsel. Anything else you use, a balloon, a rolled-up newspaper, just doesn't give that satisfying crack.

It's probably from the Courtroom that the famous "Pay the Two Dollars" gag came from, although burlesque might have stolen it from vaudeville. This is the situation where the victim has a $2 parking ticket— and an ambitious defense attorney. The Judge orders him to pay the $2 and the defense counsel is furious. He screams at the Judge and the Judge gets angry . . . and meanwhile the nervous victim is muttering to his attorney: "Pay the two dollars."

Too late, the Judge rules them in contempt of court and the victim must serve ninety days in jail or pay a $200 fine. But the defense attorney is not done yet. "I'll appeal!" And he goes to higher and higher courts, each time the sentence getting heavier and heavier, with the victim pleading into

the crazy attorney's ear: "Pay the two dollars!" It usually ends with a life sentence!

The basic version we used is one called "It's a Wise Child." Before we got to our main scene we threw in a number of other cases which were in effect blackouts. For example, an Indian comes into court, claiming his wife has committed adultery. In fact, her child is not an Indian. The Indian dramatically sums up his appeal:

"When Indian plant corn,
      Indian get corn.
When Indian plant wheat,
      Indian get wheat.
But when Indian plant child,
      Indian get Chinaman???"

After a few blackouts like this, and various fol-de-rol such as the Judge instructing the Cop to bring in the next case, and the Cop staggering in with a case of whiskey, we move to "It's a Wise Child."

A very pretty blonde comes in and takes the witness stand. Chaos breaks loose as she arranges her skirt above her knees, and the attorneys, the Cop, and the Judge break their backs to get a good peek. This is another case of paternity; the question being—who is the father of the lady's child? All sorts of accusations are made—suspicion

even moves to the Prosecuting Attorney who admits he took the lady for a drive in a park.

"What happened?" asks the lecherous Judge.

"We made love on the back seat!"

The Court is at complete attention. The Judge says, "You made love on the back seat?"

"That's right. We made love on the back seat. And when we finished, the car was gone. We had to leave the seat in the woods."

(This gag was shamelessly stolen from Peter Arno's celebrated cartoon in the New Yorker—but in burlesque we were always very generous in drawing from all sources.)

Now it looks as if the Prosecuting Attorney is guilty, but the Judge renders a Solomon-like decision: "It's a wise child that knows its own father," he says. "Let's ask the child."

The Policeman then brings in the child—and what a child! She's a seventeen-year-old beauty with a forty-inch bust. A knockout.

"This is the child?" asks the Judge. He eyes her bosom and makes his first judicial pronouncement: "Look at those balloons!"

Now the suspense mounts as the Judge asks the child to tell the court who her father is, relying on her intuition. The Prosecuting Attorney? The girl nods "No." The Defense Counsel? No. The addled Cop? No.

"Then who is your father?" explodes the Judge.

"YOU!" she points to the Judge, and the Judge faints!

Fireman, save my wife!
This scene is the story of a fireman and his wife—
and an amorous Fire Chief. Every time the fireman is about to
make love to his wife, there is a mysterious fire alarm
that sends the fireman pell-mell into his clothes
and out the door. And at that moment
the Fire Chief steps out of the bedroom closet.

The Crazy House

Everyone loves the Crazy House. The concept is hilarious, to begin with. A man is hired as a night watchman in an Insane Asylum.

But first, a medical examination by a crazy Doctor, with his hair up in a point so that he looks like a refugee from a duck farm. The Watchman mentions this, and the Doctor gives the inevitable retort: "What do you think I am? A quack?"

The Doctor asks him how old he is.

"Forty-nine years."

"How long have you been out of work?"

"Forty-nine years."

"What's your father's name?"

"Ben."

"What's your mother's name?"

"Anna."

"What is your name?"

"Ben-Anna!"

And the Doctor concludes this probing into the watchman's family background with the question:

"Do you have a Fairy Godmother?"

"No. We've got an uncle we're not sure about!"

The medical part of the examination is brief. The Doctor taps the stethoscope at the top of the Watchman's chest, then the middle of the chest, then the bottom of the chest, saying: "Eeny-meeny-mighty Moe."

The Watchman stops the stethoscope at the belt level and says:

"Stay away from Little Joe."

The Doctor concludes that the Watchman is medically sound, and the Nurse takes over. This Nurse is fantastic. For one thing, every time she finishes a speech she does a bump and grind that almost knocks the Watchman off the stage. She asks the Watchman to undress, while she makes up the little cot which guards the door. The Watchman is embarrassed, he doesn't want to get undressed in front of a lady.

"Oh, that's all right," she says. "I'm used to those little things!"

The Watchman says: "You've been reading my mail."

But finally in a long white nightgown he gets into bed for a restful night, guarding the door at an Insane Asylum. The Nurse warns him not to let any of the patients escape. "And if you want anything," she says, executing a classic bump and grind, "just send for me!"

The Watchman lies down, and from then on it's pandemonium with never a letup. In the many various versions of the Crazy House, hundreds of different jokes and sight gags have been used.

For example, a man looking like a corpse staggers into the room. He lurches toward the comic. "Did you see a funeral go by?"

"No. Why?"

"I just fell out of the hearse!"

A man races across the stage, carrying a roll of toilet paper.

The watchman shouts, "Where are you going?"

The man holds the toilet paper up. "Crap game."

A man chases a girl through the room; a little blonde comes in with a watering can to water her garden, and deluges the comic; an enormously sexy girl comes on stage and says, "Oh, John, lay it on the floor." She does a bump, moves to another position and says, "Oh, John, lay it on the floor." She does another bump and repeats again, "Oh, John, lay it on the floor."

The watchman says, "My luck . . . my name is George."

Minnie

*This classic scene has been made fa-
mous by Harry Conley, who has been
doing it for sixty years. Harry plays
the yokel from the country; his wife
never says a word during the scene.
She stands there, stone-faced, while
Harry prowls around her, and bawls
her out. And what a bawling out! Here
are a few highlights.*

HARRY: I know your trouble! I know
what's wrong with you. But you won't
listen. . . . You're drinking too damn
much *PRUNE JUICE!*

I'm tired of standing on corners waiting for you. Why the Hell don't you order
a root beer float or something?

If you go to cross a street, why don't
you cross? First you're on one side of
the street, then on the other, then you're
in the middle of the street, going back
and forth. "There's a red light, there's
a green light, there's a taxi cab!" running
back and forth doing your damdest . . .
to get me killed! I know what you're
after. You don't fool me. You're trying
to get that *hundred-dollar* insurance
policy!

You walk down the street; everybody's
looking at you, everybody's laughing.
Making a damn fool out of yourself and

Poor Minnie
Minnie is the frozen-faced wife
who never utters a word while Harry
Conley reminds her of her flaws.

me, too. You and your ... ingrown knees! You walk like you've got diaper rash!

I tried to help you, I got you a good job, down at the winery, stomping grapes with your feet. And you got *fired!* Sitting down on the job!

I sent you for a check-up. I didn't think there was one damn thing wrong with you when I sent you to the doctor. But the minute you walked into the doctor, he told you you should go to the mountains for your kidneys. (*imitates her voice*) "I didn't know they were up there!"

What in the hell do you think about when you say those things!

Then when you come back from the doctor, calling up the doctor, don't know what you're saying over a telephone. Calls up the doctor, she says, "Doctor, would you look around your office and see if you can find my panties!"

Doctor came back to the phone, he says, "I've looked every place and I can't find your panties."

"Then I must have left them at the *dentist!*"

I'll hit you so damn hard on top of your head I'll knock your eyeballs so far down in your stomach you'll have to take your pants off to see where you're going.

The Schoolroom

This is the scene made famous by Lou Costello. The schoolteacher is a beautiful girl, armed with a folded-up bundle of papers which she bangs over the skulls of the students when they say something funny. The students are two grown men in shorts, and two phenomenally dumb girls. Their byplay brings in verses and jokes so old you may shudder, while laughing. And the sight of the teacher banging the student over the head only makes it funnier. Here it is:

TEACHER: Good morning, children.

CHILDREN: Good morning, teach.

TEACHER: Lou, why are you late?

LOU: I was parking cars all night. Made four hundred dollars.

TEACHER: Four hundred dollars? How did you make that much?

LOU: Sold one of the cars!

(*The other comic, let's call him Bud, now chimes in.*)

BUD: Hey, teach, got a little number I made up last night.

TEACHER: All right, go ahead.

BUD:
Nellie wore a little dress
It was really very thin
When she asked me how I liked it
I answered with a grin:

(*Sings*) "Wait till the sun shines, Nellie!"

(*Bang! The teacher hits him over the head.*)

BUD: Hey, teach, want to come to dinner tonight? I've got a canary that eats beans.

TEACHER: Why beans?

BUD: Wants to be a thunderbird!

(*Lou gets into the act.*)

LOU: I love breans — breans for breakfast, breans for lunch ...

TEACHER: Not breans ... beans. Watch your diction. How now brown cow?

LOU: Same way, black bull!

TEACHER: Bud, I want you to stand up and spell "Mississippi."

BUD: (*stands up*) Mississippi. Let's see. EMMY comes first, then I come. And then ESSY comes twice, I come again. And then ESSY comes twice, I PEEPEE twice, and I come again!

TEACHER: Lou, stand up and spell "cat."

LOU: You give me all the hard ones. Cat ... C—A—T.

TEACHER: Male or female?

LOU: Show me the cat!

TEACHER: (*to one of girls*) Betty, stand up and spell "Peter."

GIRL: Peter! P—Y—X ... (*she starts again*) P—I—P ... (*stops*) That's too long for me.

BUD: That will be the day!

TEACHER: Now we'll go on to our poetry. Betty, do you have a poem for us?

BETTY: Yes, I do.

"Here's to the man who loves
    his wife,
And loves his wife alone
For there's many a man loving
    another man's wife
When he should be loving
    his own."

LOU: (jumps up) That's not the way we say it in Chicago!

TEACHER: How do we say it in Chicago?

LOU:

"Here's to the man who rocks
    his child,
And rocks his child alone.
For there's many a man rocking
    another man's child,
When he thinks he's rocking
    his own."

TEACHER: Mary, do you have a poem?

MARY: Yes, teacher.

"There was a little girl from
    Boston, Mass.
Who went into the water up to
    her . . . ankles."

TEACHER: That doesn't rhyme.

LOU: It will . . . when the tide comes in!

BUD: Hey, teach, I've got one!

"There was once a young girl named
    Pat.
She gave birth to triplets, Tim, Tom,
    and Tat.
There was fun in the breeding,
But woe in the feeding,
When she found out she had no tit
    for tat."

TEACHER: Bud, stand up and give me a sentence using the word "ascot."

BUD: The cow jumped over the fence and got its ascot!

TEACHER: Betty, stand up and give us a sentence using the words "Damon and Pythias."

BETTY:

Damon and Pythias were always
    around.
Wherever Damon was, Pythias could
    be found.
One day Pythias called Damon a
    skunk,
So Damon went out and got Pythias
    drunk!

And so the gags and verses went, with the teacher banging skulls and trying to keep order in this most uncommon of schoolrooms.

The Music Teacher

This scene is uncontrolled pandemonium at its best. Its concept is marvelous. A music teacher, clutching a ukelele, and attired in tails and white Union suit drawers, greets the wildest three students in history. The first student who enters is a girl. For a music teacher, she presents problems, because she is deaf and dumb! The second student is a hard-of-hearing, eighty-year-old man with a long, white beard and a huge ear trumpet. The third student comes on stage in a sport coat—and nothing else. The coat is long, fortunately. But with his chest hair showing, and bare legs, he seems like a wild man temporarily let loose to drive the music teacher insane.

At the beginning, the music teacher, clutching a ukelele, explains that he conducts a music class. In comes the deaf and dumb girl, and the music teacher begins to sense trouble. He finally orders her to sit down while he makes up his mind how to teach her. Then comes the old man with the ear trumpet, and things really liven up. The music teacher wants no part of an old man with an ear trumpet, especially with a deaf-and-dumb girl already sitting there.

TEACHER: You're in the wrong place, old man.

OLD MAN: A-a-a-a-a-a-y?

TEACHER: I said you're in the wrong place!

OLD MAN: A-a-a-a-a-a-y?

TEACHER: (*furiously points at the ear trumpet*) Stick it in your ear! I said you're in the wrong place.

OLD MAN: Yes, you do have a funny face!

TEACHER: You're in the wrong place, this is a music store.

OLD MAN: Yes, I came in the door.

TEACHER: I don't care if you broke it down!

OLD MAN: A-a-a-a-a-a-a-y?

TEACHER: Stick it in your ear! . . . Not my ear! Your ear! We teach the ukelele. First lesson, five dollars; second lesson, three dollars; you get the third lesson free.

OLD MAN: Oh, I'll take the third lesson first!

TEACHER: How'd you hear that?

OLD MAN: A-a-a-a-a-a-y?

TEACHER: Oh, sit down! (*a knock at the door*)

OLD MAN: Somebody's knocking at the door.

TEACHER: How'd you hear that?

OLD MAN: A-a-a-a-a-a-y?

(*In comes the big man in sport coat and bare legs, holding a trombone. His first words indicate more trouble of another sort. He has a hare-lip.*)

HARE-LIP: Is nis de music store?

OLD MAN: A-a-a-a-a-a-y?

TEACHER: (*to Old Man*) Shut up! (*looks at hare-lip man*) This is the result of a pill that didn't work.

HARE-LIP: Is nis de music store?

TEACHER: This is a music class, we teach the ukelele.

HARE-LIP: Oh, no. I don't want to learn that.

TEACHER: Why not?

HARE-LIP: (*holds up trombone*) I want to play on my hambone.

TEACHER: I think you've been playing on your hambone too much!

OLD MAN: A-a-a-a-a-a-y?

TEACHER: Shut up! (*to hare-lip*) Oh, I know what you said. *Trombone!*

HARE-LIP: Nat's it. Nat's it!

TEACHER: Would you like to take a lesson now?

HARE-LIP: Why yure! Yat's what I'm here for!

TEACHER: (*imitates him*) OK. *Snit* down.

HARE-LIP: (*furious*) Just a moment, you. ARE YOU MOCKING ME?

TEACHER: (*imitates him*) Are you nidding? I wouldn't mock you. When I was born, I was very young, and my mother said *snomething* was wrong with me. She said I had an impediment in my *'peech.* And *snometimes* when I get around *snomebody* like you, I don't know what the hell I'm saying.

HARE-LIP: Oh, you poor man. I feel *snorry* for you.

TEACHER: Well, I feel sorry for you, too.

HARE-LIP: You can go see my doctor.

TEACHER: Is he good?

HARE-LIP: Is he good? . . . *HE CURED ME!*

OLD MAN: A-a-a-a-a-a-y?

TEACHER: Shut up!

HARE-LIP: (*to Old Man*) He's going to teach me how to play on my hambone.

OLD MAN: A-a-a-a-a-a-y?

HARE-LIP: He's going to teach me to . . . (*turns to teacher*) What the hell's the matter with him?

TEACHER: Stick it in his ear!

HARE-LIP: (*does a double-take at double-entendre*) Oh, no! He wouldn't like yat!

TEACHER: Well, he can't hear *without* it!

HARE-LIP: Well, he can't hear *with* it!

TEACHER: Ok, I'll stick it in for you. Hey, you old fossil. Stick it in your ear.

OLD MAN: A-a-a-a-y!

TEACHER: A-a-a-y yourself. Stick

it in your ear. Park it in the hole. (*the Old Man puts the trumpet to his ear*)

HARE-LIP: (*talks into the trumpet*) Hey, he's going to teach me how to play on my hambone.

OLD MAN: A-a-a-a-a-y.

HARE-LIP: He's . . . going . . . to . . . teach . . . me . . . how . . . to . . . play . . . oh, ptooey! (*he spits into the trumpet*)

(*The Old Man stands up with his palms upward thinking it's raining!*)

HARE-LIP: Snay, he can't hear!

TEACHER: That's what I said, stupid. He can't hear.

HARE-LIP: H–E–R–E.

TEACHER: It is not H–E–R–E. It's H–E–A–R . . . Hear!

HARE-LIP: Oh no. The *A* is silent as the *T* in fish!

TEACHER: There's no *T* in fish.

HARE.LIP: (*literally explodes in teacher's face, causing his wig to fly off in the breeze*) Tuna fish!

OLD MAN: A-a-a-a-ay?

TEACHER: (*Picking up his wig*) Oh shut up! . . . Now, let's begin the music lesson. (*he points to cute deaf and dumb girl at the other end of the row*) I'm going to give that little lady her first piece!

HARE-LIP: (*looks at teacher and girl who is five feet away*) You're going to give that girl her first piece? . . . From over here? . . . *Hello, King Kong!*

BLACKOUT

Robbery for a cause
Charlie Robinson's big pantomime scene in the show, *This Was Burlesque*, was "The Safe," and it brought howls of laughter from every audience. The concept was simple, and pure burlesque. Charlie was a drunk who staggered into a bar, made passes at a beautiful girl, and drove the bartender to distraction. In the midst of it all, his pants kept falling down, leaving Charlie shuddering in his shorts. In the end he breaks into the safe—and steals a safety pin!

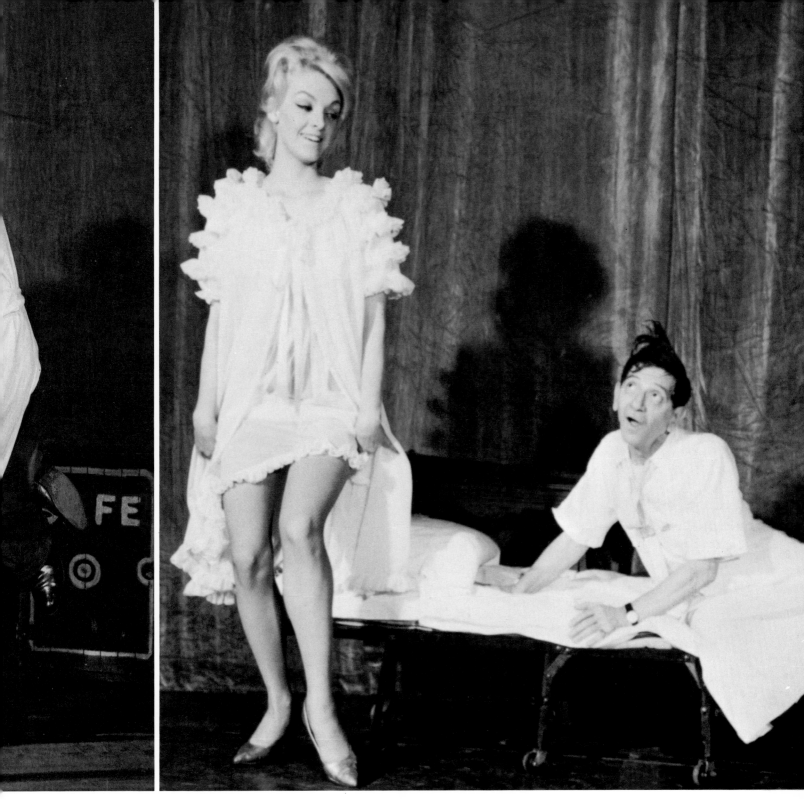

Too much for Charlie
This scene is so funny in concept that burlesque experts say
almost anybody could get a laugh playing in it. But perhaps no one was
ever funnier in the act than Charlie Robinson, because
he looked so frail and puny—and the story has to do with two
young and eager beauties who are after Charlie's body.
After a series of love sessions off stage, one after the other, poor Charlie
is carried back on stage in a wheelbarrow, a crumpled ruin of a man.

The decline and fall of burlesque

Those jolly censors

I LOVE TO TALK ABOUT CENSORS. CENSORS are crazy. For one thing, they're human—and censors should be robots. All of the censors I ever met were almost too human.

The happiest man in Boston for two decades was the censor. It was customary for him to catch the first show at the Old Howard on opening day, the Monday matinee. This particular censor was a balding fellow, plump and on the shortish side. But he knew his business. The idea was that he would stand in the wings with a pad of paper, and take notes on offensive jokes, lack of G-strings, and other moral flaws in the performance.

In those days you couldn't show any skin in Boston, as the girls would say. The management would provide us with a one-piece union suit, and we'd wear panties and bra over that. Of course, as soon as the censor left, the tights would come off and, in the case of some girls, the panties and bra, too. I'm sure the censor knew we flew out of that union suit as soon as he left, but he didn't care. He had done his duty, and he had had his thrill.

This particular censor had a great time. He planted himself right at the entrance to the stage from the wings. There happened to be an electrician's

board there, complete with the house electrician—and they took up half the space. The censor took up the other half. This meant that every time a stripper or chorus girl made her way on stage, her hefty bosoms passed right by the censor's eyes. He saw more twin peaks than Tiger Tenzing, but he never quailed in his pursuit of duty—nor did he move. From twelve till two, it was censor time in the wings, and no censor ever got closer to his job.

Once that jolly fellow had departed, there was still trouble to be expected. For Boston was a rabbit warren of censors; almost every citizen believed he was a voluntary member of the Watch and Ward Society. But luckily the management of the Old Howard knew the amateur censors to look out for, and they took precautions.

To enter the Old Howard you went up four steps to the ticket seller in the lower lobby, then you had to climb a long stairway up to the auditorium. The ticket taker standing at the top of the stairs was the most important person in the theatre. It was his responsibility to recognize every censor. I don't know how he did it, but—with one exception—he never failed. As soon as he saw the censor coming up the stairs he pressed his foot on a pedal. On stage, the show

might be in full production. A stripper might be giving her all for mankind, shimmying and grinding. Clothes might be flying in all directions. The crowd would be yelling, "Take it off!" and the music might be crashing to a crescendo. Suddenly, a red light would start blinking in the footlights. A censor had arrived.

Imagine Mickey Mantle trying to stop in the middle of his swing. That's what those stormy strippers would have to do. I particularly think of Georgia Sothern, whose act built up in momentum until it was almost impossible to stop. Red light! Hold it! The hips would stop as if paralyzed. The clothes would come flying back from the wings. The perspiring musicians would dissolve to a waltz. And by the time the censor reached the top of the stairs and looked down at the stage he would see—not a hip-swinging, hair-tossing, half-naked tigress—but a nun on a casual stroll through a most unlikely convent. Or so the angelic Georgia would look when the red light cast its glow, and she would demurely finish her act, fully dressed.

The only time I personally know that the censor-watcher failed in his job was on one of my appearances. I never once was in a show that was raided. The censors all knew my act was innocent, at least in comparison to the others they saw. But sometimes a show would be raided because someone other than the star dared to take off too much—or even if the comics got out of hand. I always censored my own shows, but when the cat's away, those little burlesque mice will play. And that's just what happened on this historic night.

The Police Commissioner of Boston at the time was a handsome bachelor named Joe Timulty. He later became famous as Joe Kennedy's companion, but in those days he was a buddy of mine. Joe loved to dance. He'd pick me up after the show each evening in a limousine, chauffered by a police sergeant. People thought I was being arrested every night. Then we'd go to a place like the roof top of the Ritz-Carlton to dance. And that's where we were the night the Old Howard was raided. You can imagine it made funny headlines. *"Ann Corio dancing with Police Commissioner while her show was raided."*

It only made him more popular. And it saved me from an appearance in court, which I wouldn't have liked. In later years I've thought of that incident, and I often wonder whether he took me dancing that night just to make sure I wasn't caught in that raid. As the girls say, it helps to have friends—especially Police Commissioners.

But Boston wasn't the only place we were threatened by censors. No indeed. In Worcester, Massachusetts, a censor came backstage and started to berate me for not wearing enough. It made me furious because my mother happened to be visiting backstage that night, and heard the man. Then this hardworking censor followed me into my dressing room, still arguing, locked the door—and asked for a closer look at my bosom. In other words, he wanted to berate me by using the braille system. A knocking at the door saved me. It was my mother following up her look-a-but-no-touch rule. That censor took off under a barrage of Italian—and I never saw him again in the theatre. Come to think of it, maybe he wasn't a censor!

When I left burlesque for other fields, I still had trouble with the censors sometimes. I remember one night in Cambridge, Massachusetts, when I was appearing in my favorite role as Tondelayo in *White Cargo*. All I wore in this play was a loincloth and a pound of brown powder. This was not enough. For after the performance I was visited in my dressing room by the censor, and two policemen. I kept slapping that powder on me while they talked, and I soon had them choking to death. But, while these policemen were so occupied in my dressing room, the box office up front was robbed! Two policemen inside the theatre, and the box office gets held up. That made some faces red. But I went along with the censor, at least. The next performance I wore *a pound and a half* of brown powder.

The name's La Guardia

IN 1967, THIRTY YEARS AFTER BURlesque was banned from New York for indecency, *This Was Burlesque* opened in Las Vegas. The day after the opening one of our employees was in the gambling salon and overheard two people talking about our show.

"What did you think of it?" one of them asked the other.

"The jokes were funny. But I was disappointed."

"Why?"

"It's the *tamest* show in town."

I knew what he meant, because the night before I had attended the *Lido* show. At least fifty girls, bare from the waist up, paraded and danced and flirted with the audience. Burlesque, that frowned-upon, denounced-in-pulpit, blasted-by-politician villain of thirty years ago, was now "tame." But, oh, in 1937! What a difference three decades make.

I have never been one to defend the sins of burlesque in that period. There were indeed sins in the area of good taste, and I'm going to mention some of them; but the severity of the condemnation, and the outright banning of *all* burlesque instead of just a few shoddy operators, far exceeded the crime.

I have another problem in writing this chapter. Mayor La Guardia was — and is — my favorite politician of all times. Jim Curley was nice — but Fiorello was an Italian, and we Italians stick together like good *pasta*. Fiorello — and his License Commissioner, Paul Moss — had good reason to be provoked. The trouble really was that people liked burlesque, and in the thirties they were flocking to the shows. What this meant was that more and more theatres sprang up, and more and more competition flared up between the operators. On 42nd Street burlesque houses were

"Me Tondelayo. Make you very happy."

all over the place, each one fighting for the customers. Part of the battle was also carried on in the front of the theatres with pictures and posters of girls in their nature suits.

Minsky is a name as closely associated with burlesque as Gypsy or myself. The fabulous Minsky family has been in the business since the twenties. At this time, they were still operating theatres, and the wrath of the public commissioners fell mostly on them because their name was so famous.

From time to time they would try to cool down their shows and advertising, but soon, under competition, they would revert to the billboards that were causing a lot of the trouble.

In those days Times Square was the magnet for the tourists. Millions of them visited New York each year, and they all had to see the Square. Reporters on newspapers such as the *Mirror* pointed out that the tourists' first impression of New York was a center of sin, with huge billboards of naked girls staring them in the face.

Meanwhile, inside the show, the operators were encouraging the girls to get more and more daring. Later on this technique backfired on them when they attempted to clean up the shows under the eye of the city's censors. But

for a while it brought increasingly more steamy-eyed patrons into the theatres.

Clergymen thundered from the pulpits with the same bolts from Heaven that had showered the British Blondes decades before. The newspapers, sensing a popular issue, took up the hue and cry and called for action.

And in the early thirties, they got it— but never quite enough. Mayors before La Guardia attempted to revoke the licenses, but they always lost in court, because most of burlesque comedy is double-entendre, and there was always an explanation from the glib comics. I know, because I've fought with comics for years about different lines, but they've always looked shocked, as if only I, with my vulgar mind, could possibly understand the joke in the wrong way.

The periodic raids on the strippers always resulted in a girl with a very modest dress appearing quietly before a judge and denying everything. Burlesque also had its supporters in such organizations as the National Council of Freedom from Censorship. With all this, burlesque still had its troubles and in 1933 was banned for the first time. But it didn't stick, because the operators shrewdly called in an old and respectable name. None other than

Sam Scribner who had run the Columbia Wheel so cleanly that vaudeville almost ruined it. Sam was appointed as mediator, and under his guidance a compromise was worked out. From now on the girls would wear net brassieres and panties.

The period of goodwill lasted a little while, but soon those operators were scrambling for the buck. Even those who weren't, those who tried to keep their shows clean, had their troubles with the girls whom they had encouraged just a few years ago to go all the way.

One stripper nearly drove her stage manager mad. He was determined that none of his girls would reveal enough to cause a raid on his theatre, but this star fooled him every time. She wore what we call a "Chicago G-string" which is a now-you-see-it, now-you-don't G-string. To be honest with you I'm not sure how the trick was done. All I know is that the G-string was not sewn to the elastic in the regular way.

Before every performance, the stage manager would personally examine the stripper just before she went on stage for her number. The girl would pick up her dress, and there would be the G-string. But, when she got out on stage and started into her number, the G-

The "Little Flower"
Fiorello H. La Guardia was elected mayor of New York City on a reform platform, and before long he clamped down on burlesque.

BURLESQUE DEAD, SAYS LAGUARDIA

HARRIED into fighting mood by strip-tease burlesque promoters' "brazen and arrogant attitude of defiance," Mayor LaGuardia announced yesterday that the "art" which made Broadway notorious, is dead. And that there will be no revival.

With the doors of every burlesque theatre in the city closed and irate owners scheduled to appear in Supreme Court today in an effort to force renewal of their licenses, Mayor LaGuardia dampened their spirits thus:

"There will be no let-up on the part of the city in this situation. It will be a bitter fight to the finish against incorporated filth!"

Mayor LaGuardia denounced activities of the city's burlesque barons and indicated he stood squarely behind Police Commissioner Lewis J. Valentine, who charged that the strip-tease rage is largely responsible for the current wave of sex crimes.

He revealed that city officials had bided their time, awaiting Friday's zero hour (license renewal time) to strike. Said he:

"Since the decision of the Court of Appeals, which curtailed our powers, the city waited patiently for renewal time.

"Operators of burlesque houses, meanwhile, put more and more filth and lewdness into their productions and have maintained a brazen and arrogant attitude of defiance."

TWO COURT CASES

The Mayor's venom was evoked by actions of two burlesque operators—those of the Eltinge and Gaiety Theatres—who went before Supreme Court Justice Edgar Lauer Saturday and obtained a

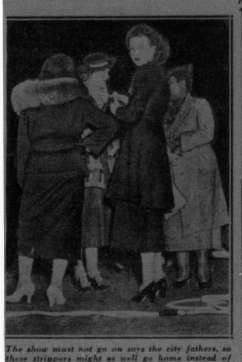

The show must not go on says the city fathers, so these strippers might as well go home instead of hanging around the Irving Place Burlesque. Many artistes are contemplating going on relief.

string wasn't there: it had disappeared. When she got back to the wings there would be the manager screaming, "I saw it! I saw it!" But the stripper would show him the G-string still in place, and he could do nothing but scream and pray.

So the shows again became as raunchy as ever, and once again the newspapers and clergy were throwing thunderbolts at City Hall, and in the midst of it all, Fiorello H. La Guardia was elected.

His License Commissioner, Moss, was a theatrical operator in his own right.

He didn't like burlesque, possibly because his brother ran a legitimate theatre nearby. At least that was Abe Minsky's allegation. More likely he felt that the crowd of burlesque theatres in the heart of the city, with their ever-more-daring shows, really needed to be cleaned up. Or cleaned out.

That clever stripper and her Chicago G-string were the first to go down the chute. The Irving Place Theatre, in which her act was headlined, was raided almost immediately. The operator of the theatre personally appealed to Mayor

La Guardia, and promised to tidy up his show. The Mayor knew that the closing of burlesque in New York would throw thousands of people out of work so he gave the owner a chance.

But another operator really pulled the plug out. Not only did he keep his shows as dirty as before, but he sent someone out to the high schools to give "twofers" to the kids.

Mayor La Guardia said that this was the end—everybody out of the pool!

There was another raid, this time on the New Gotham Theatre, and another

Strippers at the bar
Burlesque in New York had been meeting its competition by getting naughtier and naughtier, when Mayor La Guardia decided to take action under the obscenity laws. Soon police paddy wagons were filled with stripteasers on their way to appearances in court.

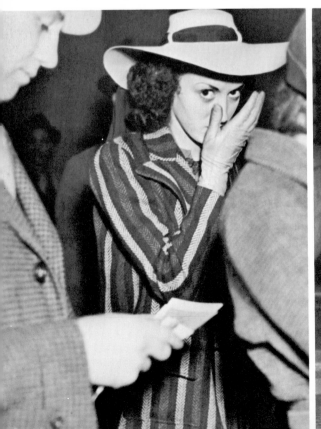

headline trial, but La Guardia was determined now. The trial was won, and Moss immediately moved to close the theatres. On May 2, 1937, burlesque came to an end in New York.

What caused the death of burlesque? It's an old story in show business. Whenever someone comes up with a good thing, other profiteering types will attempt to copy it, outdo it, and eventually ruin it. It's happening today. If there's a good show on television one year, the next season there will be three copies of it, and the public will get sick of all four, including the original. A good movie will have three imitations or more so quick you can't sell the first.

Burlesque was, and is, a good thing. Its merits have been proved by our revival. But the copies of burlesque on Times Square with everything done to excess were miserable. Those shows should have been banned. I agreed with Mayor La Guardia. Burlesque operators tried to keep their theatres open with a perversion of burlesque called, of all things, "vaudesque." I suppose they meant sexy vaudeville, but as they were prohibited from being sexy, they ended up being just plain vaudeville, and not very good vaudeville at that. The public didn't buy it. I know, because I was one of the first performers the theatre owners called in to try to save their financial lives. They knew that La Guardia and Moss respected me for non-vulgar shows. As a result, within weeks of the ban, there was my name in eight-foot letters on Times Square. The operators were allowed to bill their shows as "Follies." And that's just what they were. They all lost their shirts, and that

Don't you dare move!
To avoid bans, burlesque producers
tried different types of shows.
In some cities, girls could pose nude—
but they couldn't move a muscle.

was the only thing allowed to come off.

I appeared at the Apollo Theatre on 42nd Street in a black chiffon gown with a huge lock on my back and sang a touching song, "I would if I could, but I can't." Then I did a sketch with Joey Faye in which I came out as a widow and sang "Mr. Striptease is dead!" And Joey was carried on stage on a board as Mr. Striptease.

Joey and I also did a funny Romeo and Juliet scene—the balcony scene, of course. But we couldn't use any indecent lines because the censors, who were watching this show as no show had ever been watched before, would be on us in a minute. So we played the scenes exactly as Shakespeare had written them—every verse, every line, every word from the pen of the Great Bard. But we changed the moves and put in some gestures. For example, when Shakespeare declaimed about a "cheek" my *derriere* was in front of Romeo's bulging eyes.

Predictably the censors were backstage when we finished. But old Joey had a well-thumbed copy of Shakespeare and he showed them the lines, and what could they do? We were probably the most unusual Shakespeare repertory company ever to perform.

Fenced in
It's all over in New York as
a fence goes up around Minsky's—
and an era ends for burlesque.

"Jungle Siren"
Ann Corio appears in a poster
typifying her brief career
as a star of low-budget movies.

But the fans at that theatre had been accustomed to seeing stronger stuff than Shakespeare. A decade of going-too-far on stage had changed not only burlesque, but its loyal fans. The boys who used to go "to see the comics" were no longer there. Burlesque, the burlesque that I love, was dead in New York. It should have been listed as a suicide.

What happened to me? The road was still open, and I could have gone on touring for big money. But just at this point, Hollywood called. The time seemed ripe. Burlesque was going into a decline. I, however, was healthy. And I had always wanted to be an actress. Visions of MGM danced in my head. Million-dollar contracts, Cecil B. De-Mille spectacles, white limousines and sables and dressing rooms marked "Star."

It didn't work out quite that way. You've heard of low-budget movies. The movies I was hired to play were so low-budget they didn't have enough money to finish them. To make it worse, what I had thought would be my first chance to exhibit my talents while dressed turned out to be a false illusion, too. My producers took care of that in a hurry. They starred me in jungle pictures, and my sarong looked like Dorothy Lamour's handkerchief. In later years,

interviewers have asked me about my Hollywood experiences. I always tell them my pictures weren't released, they escaped! They would plan a one-week shooting schedule. If the picture wasn't finished at the end of that week, they'd just wrap it up right there and send it out to my adoring public without an ending. Of course, the plots were so crazy you couldn't even tell the beginning, let alone the ending. They didn't want them good, they wanted them Tuesday.

To make these silly pictures, they paid me $10,000 a week. This was probably more than the rest of the budget com-bined. But after a while I couldn't take it anymore—I don't mean the money, but the pain. In the East, burlesque was dying. And in the West, my fabulous film career was limping to a tree-lined halt in its last studio jungle.

And thus the history of burlesque might have closed, with just a few tattered remnants of shows in forlorn theatres in dingy areas of industrial towns.

Except for one thing. I had an idea. It took me almost twenty years to bring it to fruition, but then I never was a fast worker. And there were a few obstacles. Like everyone was against me.

Burlesque returns

FOR TWENTY YEARS, BURLESQUE WAS IN the doldrums after Mayor La Guardia's edict. Many theatres in cities such as Washington, Philadelphia and Boston remained in business, but the pall cast by the Little Flower's condemnation affected every corner of burlesque. Gradually, the great strippers deserted the burlesque stage. Attendance fell off, and theatres passed out of the hands of the competent operators into shoddier hands that tended to make dirty everything they touched.

Competition sprang up in nightclubs, such as those on New York's West 52nd Street, and in seedier sections everywhere. Literally thousands of girls were stripping in clubs where the runways ran right past the eyes of the drunken customers. These shows featured a dreary parade of so-called strippers, with only a loud MC to break the tedium. No comics—and the girls were usually third-rate. But then they were closer to the customer than the girls on the burlesque stages, and a whole lot more available. So fewer and fewer people flowed through the doors of burlesque houses.

The tragic thing was that burlesque, instead of fighting back with better comedy and more beautiful girls, yielded and actually joined the competition. More and more strippers were added to the bill, and the comics really did take a back seat. The burlesque I had known was being converted into a stripper-parade. Chorus girls were eliminated. Comics were ordered to fill in just a few words between strippers. The strippers, themselves, realizing their acts couldn't compete with their nightclub sisters started calling themselves "exotics" and doing numbers with obscene props.

Living in semi-retirement in California, I suffered when I thought about it—but what could one girl do? It seemed the whole climate had changed, and that the trend was irreversible.

In 1960 I signed a contract to appear in Bristol, Pennsylvania, in a summer theatre production of *Cat on a Hot Tin Roof*. The producer was a young man named Mike Iannucci.

In newspapers, magazines, and television and radio I've been given credit for the amazing revival of burlesque. It's only natural, because I was a well-known name in burlesque, and the reporters have always been my buddies, anyway. But everyone who really knows the story is aware that Mike Iannucci really brought burlesque back to Broadway.

What makes it amusing is that Mike was the last person in the world who would have been expected to be involved in a revival of burlesque. For one thing he was too young to remember burlesque in its heyday. For another, his only background in show business was one year operating a summer stock theatre. Before that, he had been a professional football player. I've always thought it was that experience as a football player that really got us through all the obstacles we met. It all began when Mike and I were talking one night, after my performance in his theatre. We discussed the idea of bringing burlesque back to America just as it was in its heyday. Mike was enthused right off. He thought present-day audiences would love burlesque, that all of them were nostalgic for it.

I felt that way myself, but then I was too close to the subject to be sure. But here was a young fellow who was not even of the "burlesque" generation who thought it was a great idea. My hopes went up.

Mike set out to interest backers, and he raised a few thousand dollars in front money, mostly from relatives and close friends. Clutching that loot, he moved to New York—and ran into a stone wall. All the "smart" boys at William Morris, GAC, and other agencies immediately told him the sad truth. Burlesque was as out of date as a Packard roadster. Today's audiences were hip. The comedy we thought was funny was too corny for today's generation. As for strippers, girls were showing more flesh at the neighborhood movie theatre. Nothing about the idea was right. Burlesque was dead. Don't waste your money.

I had gone back to California, but now I came back to give Mike some moral assistance. I remember one big agent who kept Mike waiting for three full days in his anteroom, and never did see him. Old friends in burlesque whom I counted on for assistance backed off because they thought the idea was so worthless. Besides, there was another argument we heard time and again. Hadn't burlesque been banned from New York? We couldn't put the show on even if we could raise the money.

A theatre owner who was still a friend of mine and remembered all the money I had made for him was kind enough to advance us a few thousand dollars. But it was not enough to put on a show in New York—so we decided to try it out in a nightclub in Boston.

"Nightclub" is a generous name to give to that place. It was not by any means a big, plush establishment. To make matters worse, the owner changed

Ann in her nightclub days

the name of the club right before we opened and didn't inform the telephone company. The result was that people who heard or read about the show couldn't even find the club.

The real tragedy of this try-out, however, was the reception we got from the people who attended. We had a tiny cramped stage on a raised platform above the customers—and if there's one thing burlesque needs it's room! We couldn't afford to hire the comics we wanted. In short, the show was lousy. Applause was thinly scattered; and, even though the reviewers gave us good notices, audiences just didn't come. We were, as everyone had predicted, a flop.

Well, that was the end of that dream! I started thinking about my lovely house in Malibu, and wondering why I had ever been foolish enough to try this crazy adventure.

But then fate intervened in the guise of the poor fellow who had advanced us the front money and was seeing it go down the drain. He asked us to move the show to his burlesque theatre for a week, after the nightclub run ended. He figured my name alone would draw nostalgic fans even if the show didn't go over.

Twenty years had passed, and there I was on a burlesque stage again. And

something magical happened. The comedy scenes came alive, as the comics relaxed in a familiar atmosphere. The chorus lines broke everyone up squealing, "Hello, fellas! Would you like me to powder your back?" The audiences roared, and suddenly there was a run on the theatre. We played to packed houses night after night, and everyone in the audience seemed to be having the greatest time of his life.

That reception was like a heart transplant, and I think that the patient—burlesque—will now live for centuries. We came down from Boston with something to sell. Audiences had responded to our show. They loved burlesque. But still, the investment money was hard to find. We heard that the Phoenix Theatre on 12th Street and Second Avenue was available. It would be perfect for our show, because, among other reasons, we could produce it there for about $25,000, whereas on Broadway it might cost $500,000. Besides we felt it was the right background for our raffish show. We didn't have expensive sets and gorgeous costumes. The complete set for one of our big scenes was a wooden box with a comic sitting on it.

We budgeted at $25,000 and, believe it or not, only raised $16,000. And we put the show on, mostly through the

Man of vision
Mike Iannucci brought burlesque back to New York, and his show, *This Was Burlesque,* fooled skeptics by becoming a big hit.

189

heroic endeavors of Mike Iannucci who, when the union stagehands went home, would hang drops, hammer together sets, and do a thousand things that saved money.

But word was going through New York like a fire out of control. Old-time reporters were delighted to find I was still alive—and not living in Argentina. We got all kinds of press coverage, ranging from local newspapers to *Newsweek* magazine, before we opened.

But no one was convinced we were right, not even our own press agent, who called me up the day before the show and pleaded with me to call the whole thing off. "The show isn't ready," he said. "You'll be killed by the critics." But it was too late to stop now. We were changing scenes, sewing costumes, hanging drops practically to the last minute before the curtain went up, and the show went on.

I'll never forget that opening night. It was unlike any other opening night in New York history. We were bringing a whole era back, and for at least two-thirds of that first act, the audience seemed almost stunned. They barely laughed at some very funny scenes. Their applause was slight. Then, midway during that act, something caught on. Almost at once they appeared to relax, to realize what they were seeing.

It was not, as they seemed to suspect, a gigantic put-on. This *was* burlesque.

The audience laughed all through that second act, and then they all went home seemingly happy. But opening-night audiences are almost always happy. What would the critics say?

Well, that was the second reason this opening night was different from any other. I am absolutely sure that we are the only show in modern history to have an opening night—and not even think about the reviews. We gave a party at the apartment of one of the backers for the cast. We were having a great time— but no one even thought of going out for the newspapers, or calling anyone to find out what the reviewers would say. Don't ask me why. Even today I don't know, except for the fact it must have never occurred to us that our little show would get good reviews. How could it?

Then in the crush I heard a pretty girl answer a telephone. And I heard her say, "Joyous . . . wonderful . . . ," adjectives like that. I took the phone and found out that it was our press agent, reading the *New York Herald Tribune* review written by Judith Crist. Here is part of that review:

The joyous thing about "This Was Burlesque" is not simply that this is what it was, kiddies—but that we finally have on hand a simple, funny revue.

191

Julius Sneezer and Cleopotroast
Richard Burton and Elizabeth Taylor were making headlines
shooting *Cleopatra* in Rome, so the Ann Corio troupe
revived the classic burlesque sketch, "Julius Sneezer and
Cleopotroast." With a garbage lid for a shield, and
a kitchen spoon for a sword, Sneezer fights for Ann's love.

Saving all souls
In this skit, the preacher warns Steve Mills that the devil
awaits him inside that nightclub. Steve is impressed.
Then the devil appears in the person of blonde Nicole Jaffe,
and Steve is torn by temptation. In the end, the preacher
goes into the club himself to save the blonde's soul.

It's refreshing—and nostalgic. No beatniks, no stoolsitters, no take-offs on singers, psychiatrists, or Kennedys. Just the basics, as Ann Corio herself puts them: slapstick baggy-pants comedians and pretty girls, the former equipped with all the knowhow of a venerable trade, the latter with all that's needed in the bump-and-grind business. Leave your social conscience with the ticket-taker and enjoy.

Miss Crist continued by enumerating the virtues of our show. She wrote kind and glowing words about me and praised the strippers I introduced—Mary Alagia and Dolores Du Vaughan—the dancer-comedienne Mara Lynn and the chorus line, "whose precision is from nothing but whose enthusiasm is grand." Most of all, she enjoyed the four Top Bananas: Steve Mills, Connie Ryan, Charlie Robinson and Mac Dennison. Miss Crist's final words were reserved for the "stylish staging," the "rich costumes" and the band "that knows the exact border line between schmaltz and satire. The whole company does—and the end result is a pleasing evening of relaxed entertainment. And that's what we haven't had nearly enough of lately."

Burlesque was back. People loved it. Amazingly, not only the bald-head-row types of old, but also the highbrow intellectual publications such as *The Saturday Review* and sophisticated magazines such as *The New Yorker* raved about our show, along with *Time, Life,* *Newsweek* and practically every other national publication.

We went on to make show-business history. We played three long years on the Lower East Side, and then, instead of folding, moved up to Broadway and opened at the Hudson Theatre to another volley of great reviews. Then, we went on the road and broke every box-office record in almost every city.

With our success came the real burlesque revival, which I'll talk about in the next chapter. Great comics who had tended to play down their past in burlesque were suddenly proud of it. Television networks, which would not ever have thought of permitting it on the screen, suddenly found that when they did, the show got the highest audience rating of the whole year.

Oh, one more thing. What about the concern that New York's ban on burlesque would not let us open? In short, were we raided? Obviously not. Mayor Robert Wagner sent one of his staff to check on the show even before it opened. He reported to Wagner that by today's standards the show was innocent. And to make it all chummy, I happened to be invited to a banquet just after the show opened, and Mayor Wagner was there. He asked me to sit next to him for photographers. That act was as good as the official seal.

Girl of the Year
When *This Was Burlesque* opened in New York to great reviews, Ann Corio was chosen "Show Business Girl of the Year" by the Saints and Sinners, a theatrical fraternity. Here Miss Corio appears with Saints and Sinners celebrities Harry Hershfield (far right) and Walter Kiernan (below, left).

It's
everywhere

"HEAH COME DE JUDGE, HEAH COME DE Judge, Heah come de Judge!" It's Sammy Davis, Jr., on network television, chanting the phrase over and over again until it becomes a national password. Everybody's saying it. What does the phrase mean? It's merely the opening statement in one of the most famous burlesque scenes—"The Courtroom."

Red Skelton, every Christmas, does a scene "Trying to Get Arrested." It's a burlesque scene. Jackie Gleason has made his biggest hit with "The Honeymooners." He's done literally hundreds of shows—and they're all based on a burlesque skit, "Friendly Neighbors."

I could go on and on, but by now I think you get the idea. Burlesque comedy is a beloved form of entertainment that has woven its way into American life.

They love it. No one ever comments on an amazing fact: the most popular comedy show year after year is Red Skelton's. His show is almost straight burlesque—and it is always in the Top Ten while the "Gunsmokes" and the "Man from U.N.C.L.E.s" come and go.

After our show was produced, and favorably reviewed in national publications, the networks took what they thought was a daring step.

Bell-ringer
Phil Silvers on television and on the stage perpetuates the spirit of burlesque.

Lovable clown
Red Skelton's burlesque scene, "Trying to Get Arrested," is a hit on TV.

They allowed an ex-burlesque comic named Danny Thomas to put on a burlesque show. It was called "The Wonderful World of Burlesque." I personally didn't think that particular show was so great, but even so it got the highest audience ratings recorded that year. It was such a smash that Danny has revived it year after year.

On Broadway we had shows such as *A Funny Thing Happened on the Way to the Forum, Top Banana, Star and Garter* and many others that incorporated burlesque comedy, directly or indirectly. In fact, it's hard not to incorporate it because burlesque comedy appeals to the belly-laughers, and, believe it or not, people love a belly laugh. How subtle was Charlie Chaplin when his cane tripped up a waiter with a full tray? Yet who would not agree that Charlie is the most popular comic who ever lived. His Music Hall routines, the British equivalent of burlesque comedy, made him the lovable tramp. And every burlesque comic in baggy pants was a part of that tradition.

As for revealing the human anatomy, I don't know whether burlesque can take all the credit for that. After all, as I've pointed out elsewhere, girls have been revealing their beautiful bodies for a long, long time. But girls today are wearing miniskirts on the streets and see-through blouses to parties. Strangely enough, *I* think they're going too far—but who am I to talk? The difference is I got paid, and my tongue-in-cheek answer to reporters who ask me to drop a shoulder strap for a free press photo is always, "Not at these prices."

Yes, burlesque, that grand old show business now beginning its second century in America, is everywhere—on television, movies, the stage, and nightclubs. Its comedy is as much a part of America as apple pie. And its cheesecake is now a modern American tradition, too.

Will burlesque die again? Never, for it has never truly died. It is living today, everywhere, as it always has, in the hearts of people who want to laugh.

The Honeymooners
Jackie Gleason took his
burlesque training
into television—and
years later his famous
series, "The Honeymooners
was based on an old
burlesque scene called
"Friendly Neighbors."

A Funny Thing
Zero Mostel, who wowed
Broadway in *A Funny
Thing Happened on
the Way to the Forum,*
was pure burlesque.

Bert and Ed
Two of the greatest,
Bert Lahr and Ed Wynn,
enjoy a coffee break
backstage at NBC, before
going on television
to reveal once again
the comic genius they first
developed in burlesque.

Hold on tight!
Danny Thomas gets a
good grip on his
trousers, as Nanette
Fabray attempts to
tear them off.
It's all part of the
fun on Danny's
television show,
*The Wonderful World
of Burlesque.*

Guest star
Frank Sinatra was never in burlesque, but he was happy to appear with Danny Thomas in a classic burlesque blackout.

Nurse, nurse!
Zany Carol Channing plays the nurse, and Danny looks sick.

Guilty parties
Cyd Charisse and Silvers are guests in Danny's Hotel skit.

All together, now!
Danny's chorus
may not have been
Rockettes, but
Lee Remick
gave her all.

Crazy House revival
Mickey Rooney as
the wild doctor
lunges for the
nurse, Edie Adams.

Hoofers
Three great talents—Danny Thomas,
Phil Silvers and Tennessee
Ernie Ford—whoop it up with old-time
burlesque gusto for TV fans.

"Heah cum de judge"
Mickey Rooney is the Judge, and
Lee Remick the shapely defendant, in
this television revival of
the burlesque Courtroom scene.

Acknowledgments

The pictures reproduced in this book were obtained from the following sources. Where more than one picture appears on a page, credits are given from left to right and from top to bottom.

Page 2: Culver Pictures; **4:** Museum of the City of New York, Culver Pictures, Nick Amoresano; **5:** Culver Pictures (two), Brown Brothers, Avery Willard; **8:** Brown Brothers; **10:** Culver Pictures; **11:** Culver Pictures; **12:** The Bettmann Archive, Culver Pictures; **13:** Brown Brothers; **14:** Culver Pictures; **16:** Brown Brothers; **17:** Culver Pictures; **18:** Brown Brothers; **19:** Brown Brothers (two), Culver Pictures; **21** through **23:** Museum of the City of New York; **24** through **27:** The Woodrow Gelman Collection; **28-29:** Culver Pictures; **30:** Culver Pictures; **31:** New York Public Library; **32:** Culver Pictures, Brown Brothers (two); **33:** Culver Pictures; **35:** New York Public Library; **36:** Culver Pictures; **37:** Museum of the City of New York, Culver Pictures; **38:** Brown Brothers; **41:** Culver Pictures; **42:** The Bettmann Archive; **43:** The Bettmann Archive; **45:** Brown Brothers; **46:** Culver Pictures; **47:** Brown Brothers; **48:** The Bettmann Archive, Culver Pictures; **49:** Culver Pictures; **50:** The Bettmann Archive, Culver Pictures (two); **51:** Culver Pictures; **52:** Brown Brothers; **53:** Culver Pictures, Brown Brothers; **54:** Culver Pictures; **55:** New York Public Library; **56:** Culver Pictures; **57:** Culver Pictures; **58:** Culver Pictures; **59:** Brown Brothers; **60:** Culver Pictures; **61:** The Bettmann Archive; **63:** Culver Pictures; **64:** Culver Pictures; **65:** Culver Pictures, Brown Brothers; **66:** Culver Pictures; **67:** Culver Pictures; **68:** Brown Brothers; **69:** Culver Pictures; **72:** Culver Pictures; **73:** Culver Pictures; **75:** Culver Pictures; **77:** Wide World; **81:** Wide World; **82-83:** Bruno of Hollywood; **85:** Wide World; **87:** Culver Pictures; **88-89:** Culver Pictures; **90:** Culver Pictures; **91:** Culver Pictures; **92:** Wide World; **93:** Culver Pictures; **96-97:** Bruno of Hollywood; **99:** Culver Pictures; **100-101:** Wide World; **102:** Wide World; **105:** Culver Pictures; **108-109:** Culver Pictures; **111:** Culver Pictures; **112:** Culver Pictures; **114:** Culver Pictures; **115:** Culver Pictures; **116:** Culver Pictures, The Bettmann Archive; **117:** Culver Pictures; **118:** New York Public Library; **119:** Brown Brothers, Culver Pictures; **124-125:** Culver Pictures; **126** through **129:** Garry Winogrand, Brackman Associates; **133:** Avery Willard; **134:** The Bettmann Archive; **135:** Avery Willard; **136-137:** New York Public Library; **138** through **141:** Diane Dickerson; **142-143:** Gene Daniels, Black Star; **145:** Wide World; **146:** Culver Pictures; **149:** New York Public Library; **151:** Gene Daniels, Black Star; **159:** Wide World; **163** through **167:** Avery Willard; **168:** Diane Dickerson; **179:** Wide World; **180:** Brown Brothers; **181:** Brown Brothers; **182-183:** Wide World; **184:** New York Daily News; **186:** Bruno of Hollywood; **190-191:** Wide World; **192:** Avery Willard; **193:** Avery Willard; **196:** Culver Pictures; **198:** The Bettmann Archive; **199:** The Bettmann Archive, NBC; **200** through **205:** NBC; **207:** Diane Dickerson.